I'LL CLIMB MOUNT EVEREST ALONE

Captain Maurice Wilson, M.C.

I'LL CLIMB
MOUNT EVEREST
ALONE

The Story of Maurice Wilson

DENNIS ROBERTS

faber and faber

This edition first published in 2010
by Faber and Faber Ltd
Bloomsbury House, 74–77 Great Russell Street
London WC1B 3DA

A CIP record for this book is available from the British Library

ISBN 978-0-571-26986-0

Contents

List of Illustrations

Acknowledgments

I AM grateful for the advice and assistance of Mr. and Mrs. L. J. Evans.

The passages from works by Eric Shipton, Frank Smythe, James Ramsey Ullman and Hugh Ruttledge are quoted by kind permission of the authors (or their executors) and publishers.

I should like to thank the Royal Geographical Society for permission to reproduce photographs Nos. 12, 13, 14, 15, 16, 17 and 19.

Foreword

ALTHOUGH it is more than twenty years ago, I still have a vivid recollection of sitting with my companions under a rock at 21,000 feet in the upper basin of the East Rongbuk Glacier, while Kempson read aloud from the diary of the man whose body we had just found on the moraine a few yards away. It had been lying there for more than a year, and now it was as if the man himself was speaking to us, revealing his secret thoughts. Outside our shelter there was complete silence as the snow fell in large fluffy flakes.

As I listened to the strange, intimate story, I soon had little doubt of the writer's sincerity. The motive behind his wild venture was unusual. It was obvious that he had little liking for the mountains, and he certainly claimed no spiritual uplift in their presence. At the same time I did not feel that he was striving for personal glorification. He believed that he was guided by some kind of divine inspiration to deliver a message to humanity. His implicit faith in his destiny seems to have been with him to the last. This being the case it is obviously futile to judge his project from a mountaineering standpoint. Nor have we any touchstone by which to judge his arrogance, so clearly revealed in his diary; for this characteristic may well be essential to his kind of faith. We cannot fail to admire his courage.

ERIC SHIPTON

The greatness of mountaineering on the highest hills lies in the fact that no single man is capable of reaching a summit by his own efforts. It is this that segregates the greatest peaks of the world from peaks of less altitude. They demand much more than a personal approach.

Maurice Wilson believed that, unversed as he was in

mountaineering technique and in all the manifold problems inherent in the ascent of Everest, he could attempt that mountain alone. He believed that through faith, and faith alone, he could reach the summit. It is a magnificent philosophy, but an impractical one. On practical and humanistic grounds his forlorn attempt was open to severe criticism. It is not expedient to glorify such a wastage of life. Yet supposing that he was actuated by no sordid motives of publicity or material advancement, that in Everest he saw an idea, a means of establishing through physical toil and suffering a joyous contact with universal forces, then, while deploring his action, I cannot withhold a feeling of admiration for his purpose. It was not mountaineering, yet it was magnificent. Call it madness, call it anything you like, but is there not an element of grandeur in the thought of this young man actuated perhaps by a flame of idealism, a desire to express something, to expand consciousness, to escape from fleshly shackles, to rise above all earthly considerations, setting out alone to scale the world's highest mountain, which four elaborate expeditions of experienced mountaineers had already failed to climb? There is something magnificent in this thought, just as there is in the thought of Mallory and Irvine disappearing for ever in the clouds surrounding the final pyramid.

Sometimes men such as Wilson, deemed mad by those who judge an action by the action itself and the results of it, rather than the thoughts and motives that inspired it, try to achieve the "impossible". They die; and if failure and success are calculable in terms of life, death and concrete performance, they have failed. But only God knows whether they have really failed.

F. S. SMYTHE

Prologue

NORTH COL: MAY, 1934

A PLUME OF powder snow was streaming from the northern face of Everest. The cold at 21,000 feet was numbing and the wind tore with insensate fury round the solitary tent that was pitched a little below the North Col. Inside the tent three men were arguing; two were Sherpas, the third was an obstinate Yorkshireman who still believed that he could climb alone the remaining 8,000 feet to the summit of the highest mountain in the world.

They argued far into the night, having to shout to make themselves heard above the splitting roar of the wind. The Sherpas, born and bred in the high hills of the Himalaya, knew that the summit of Everest was beyond the reach of any of them. But the Yorkshireman was fiercely determined to go on; if he had doubts about the outcome of his lone assault he hid them behind an air of confident bravado.

"Wait here for ten days," he said at last to the Sherpas. "Then if I don't come back, return by yourselves."

And very early the next morning he set out to finish his solitary battle with Everest, carrying with him three loaves of bread, two tins of oatmeal and a small Union Jack.

The Sherpas knew that they would never see him again. But day after day, with the weather rapidly worsening, they clung to their precarious foothold at the approaches to North Col. Only when the monsoon broke, over a week later, did they return sadly to the Rongbuk Monastery; and from there news seeped out to the world that Captain Maurice Wilson, M.C. was dead.

*   *   *

So ended the most incredible story in all the eventful

history of Mount Everest; a story compounded in almost equal parts of tragedy and heroism.

It was his attempt to prove a fantastic theory that led Maurice Wilson to make his lone quixotic challenge. He was past his physical prime when he first set foot on Everest; he had an injured arm, he had no mountaineering experience, yet he tried to climb the highest mountain in the world alone. And, after overcoming the most incredible obstacles, he reached a height of some 22,000 feet. There his quest ended in a wilderness of ice and snow and tearing wind that wore out his body but never damped the flame of his spirit.

The fact that Maurice Wilson was not the first man to reach the summit of Everest is of no more consequence than the fact that Scott was not the first man to reach the South Pole. It was the manner of their failing that has won for both men a claim to immortality.

The South Pole, the summit of Everest; how much more did these two objectives symbolize to those who sought them, than mere pinpoints on the earth's surface where no man had ever stood before.

*   *   *

Maurice Wilson's executors have now for the first time made available his diaries and letters. For this we must thank them; for without their co-operation the memory of one of the most remarkable figures of our age could not have been perpetuated.

CHAPTER ONE

THE MAN

MAURICE WILSON was born in Bradford, on April 21st, 1898. He was the third of four sons born to Mark and Sarah Wilson, and his childhood was happy, with a humdrum, unexciting sort of happiness.

His father was employed at the time of his birth as a weaver's overlooker in one of the largest Bradford Mills—a responsible and well-paid position—and from his earliest years Maurice enjoyed the comfort and security of a solid middle-class home and upbringing. In later years, the Wilson family could, had they so wished, have exchanged this comfort for some degree of luxury. For Mark Wilson was a hard-working and able man, who at quite an early age became one of the directors of the Holme Topp Mill in Little Horton. But he gave much of his money away to deserving local causes and soon in the area around Bradford the Wilson family became widely known and deeply respected for their charitable works.

Maurice inherited his father's business ability and also something even more precious—his sympathy and understanding for those whose lives were less favoured by fortune than his own. Bradford, in the early years of the century, was the scene of a good deal of poverty. Mark Wilson had no wish for his young son to hide his eyes from the unhappier side of life, and the result was that Maurice conceived in the Bradford slums a depth of feeling for the world's lame ducks and underdogs that he was never to lose.

He was educated at the Carlton Road Secondary School, and soon proved himself a bright but not exceptional pupil. Physically he was strong, and the photos of him as a child depict him as a stocky, thick-set little boy with an independent air. Only in one sphere did he display any remarkable ability, and that was in his aptitude for languages; by the time he was twelve he could speak French and German with great fluency and with hardly a trace of his Yorkshire accent —this flair for quickly picking up a language was to prove of great value to him later in his journeys among the Himalaya.

Mark Wilson had spent the whole of his life in the textile industry, and naturally he hoped that Maurice's career would follow a similar pattern to his own. There was every reason to believe that this hope would have been fulfilled, had it not been for the War. In 1914 Maurice was about to start on his apprenticeship in the world of wool and cotton, when the outbreak of war altered all his plans.

The day after his eighteenth birthday he enlisted as a private in the 5th Battalion of the West Yorkshire Regiment (the Prince of Wales' Own). After a couple of months he was promoted to the rank of corporal, and his regiment was sent on special training exercises to the Yorkshire coast. The months passed slowly by; the war seemed very far away, and Wilson began to wonder if he would ever get to France. In the spring of 1917 he was nominated for a commission, and a few days before mid-summer was posted to an officer's cadet battalion at Oxford. On October 19th he was commissioned as a second lieutenant, and the following month went with his regiment to France. The West Yorkshires were thrown almost at once into the front line, as part of the 146th Infantry Brigade holding the salient around Ypres.

The horror of trench warfare affected Wilson in the same way that it affected thousands of other brave and sensitive young men—no more and no less. Within a few weeks he had aged almost beyond recognition and he was never to forget the futile and pathetic squalor of the terrible Flanders campaigns. His regiment were plunged almost at once into the fourth battle of Ypres; many of his friends were wounded and many killed.

His own military career was short but distinguished.

In the early stages of the fourth battle of Ypres the Germans, after a heavy gas and artillery barrage, managed to

Maurice Wilson . . . the soldier

Any communications on the
subject of this letter should be
addressed to :—
THE SECRETARY,
AIR MINISTRY,
GWYDYR HOUSE,
WHITEHALL,
S.W. 1.
and the following number quoted :—
241493/33/D.D.C.A.

AIR MINISTRY,
GWYDYR HOUSE,
WHITEHALL,
LONDON, S.W. 1.

15th May, 1933.

Dear Sir,

        With reference to your letter of 10th May, it is
evident that you have completely misunderstood the position.

        The recent Everest flight expedition obtained
permission to fly over Nepalese territory only after
elaborate negotiations with the Nepalese Government by the
Government of India, who required special undertakings to
be given.

        The India Office, therefore, when we wrote con-
cerning your proposed flight to Purnea, asked us to warn
you that you cannot be permitted to fly across the frontier
without the consent of the Nepalese Government which, they
added, was not likely to be forthcoming.

        For this reason it is quite impossible for the
Air Ministry to give you any encouragement with regard to
flight to Mount Everest involving crossing Nepalese
territory.

        Yours faithfully,

        F.C.L. Bertram

        Deputy Director of Civil Aviation.

M.Wilson, Esq.,
    28, Bargrange Avenue,
      Shipley,
        Yorks.

The second letter from the Air Ministry

break the allied line at several points. They fanned out towards Hazenbrouck, but were halted by the heroic stand of the English and Australians at Meteren. Here Wilson's battalion was in the thick of the savage battle for this remote little village. Wilson himself commanded a machine-gun post close to the front. As the German attack mounted in intensity, the positions to left and right of him were abandoned, and he eventually found himself isolated in front of the British line. Soon he came under heavy mortar and machine-gun fire from either flank. All his men were either killed or wounded; but Wilson himself held fast, and by a miracle, after an Allied counter-attack, emerged unscathed. It was largely through his courage and tenacity that the attacks that day on Meteren began to peter out.

For this conspicuous gallantry and devotion to duty Wilson was awarded the Military Cross. As the *London Gazette* of September 16th said, "it was owing to his pluck and determination in holding his post that the enemy attack was held up".

But by the time his award came through Wilson was in Manchester, in the Western General Hospital. On July 19th, still in the outskirts of Meteren, he was seriously wounded by machine-gun fire while leading an Allied counter-attack. A burst of bullets splayed across his left arm and chest, and he was carried, dangerously near to death, to an Advanced Casualty Station. For ten days he was too ill to move; but his splendid physique pulled him through and he was eventually moved to a Red Cross Hospital near Boulogne, and from there to Manchester.

His struggle back to health was a long and painful one. Indeed his arm never properly healed and was to trouble him for the rest of his life—though he took great pains to conceal this and few people knew of the hours of torment it gave him.

It was autumn, 1918, before Wilson was fit enough to rejoin his Battalion, which was still near the front line in Flanders. The rest of his service, up to the signing of the Armistice, was uneventful.

In July, 1919 he was demobilized and returned to his home in Bradford. He returned a restless, unsettled and vaguely unhappy man; it would have been strange indeed if after his experiences in the trenches he had done otherwise. What was strange was the fact that while other men settled down in a matter of weeks or months or years to some sort of existence which satisfied them, it took Wilson over a decade to find his niche and purpose in life; for he had somehow developed into that most difficult and complex of men—a perfectionist.

There is a saying that to be a perfectionist is to hate life. Wilson did not hate the life he returned to in Bradford; he simply found it did not satisfy him. The routine humdrum existence of day after day in a textile office soon began to pall, and after a few months he left Bradford to seek his fortune in London. There he found life more exhilarating, but not, in the end, more suited to his ideals; and after about eighteen months he followed the same course as so many other ex-servicemen in their efforts to adjust themselves to civilian life: he emigrated.

There followed a bewildering kaleidoscope of odd journeys and odder jobs. It was not that he failed at whatever he put his hand to—the truth was very often exactly the opposite—it was simply that none of his jobs appealed to him sufficiently for him to want to settle in any of them for the rest of his life. There was an indefinable something that he felt to be lacking, and he knew that without it he would never find true happiness; nor was he the man to settle for a counterfeit contentment.

He went first to America, where he spent several months in New York; but the only effect of his stay there was that a little slang became added to his already eloquent vocabulary. From there he crossed the continent to San Francisco; then he crossed the South Pacific to New Zealand. Here he stayed for several years. He spent a couple of months selling scales as a travelling salesman. He was given the recipe for a certain quack medicine, and began preparing, bottling and selling the somewhat dubious mixture. He tried his hand at farming, and his energy and common sense brought him considerable success; but at the end of eighteen months he sold his farm and moved into Wellington. Here he came closer than ever before to finding real peace of mind—albeit in a very mundane sphere. He bought up a small ladies' dress shop, and drawing on the knowledge and experience of his early years in Bradford, he achieved considerable success. His dress shop flourished; and he could, had he wished, have settled down in Wellington to a prosperous career. But suddenly and on the spur of the moment he sold out, and caught one of the Suez-routed mail boats to England.

During the voyage he took stock of his achievements to date and was not impressed. As the ship in glorious sunshine cut through the aquamarine water beyond the Great Barrier Reef, it came to him that he was as yet neither a success nor a failure: but with thirty years behind him he must surely be approaching the cross-roads that would lead him to become either the one or the other. He looked at his fellow passengers and realized that the destiny of most of them had already been mapped out: he saw sharing the deck of the mailboat, men and women who had attained wealth and power; he saw other men and women who had frittered away their opportunities and who were bereft of riches and ideas: some to be envied, the others to be pitied— or was it the other way round? He found that those who were lacking worldly riches often proved in his eyes to be more congenial company than those whom the world would call successful. He was always in peculiar sympathy with the failures and misfits of life: " 'Blessed are the poor in spirit,' " he wrote in his diary, " 'for theirs is the kingdom of heaven', and I am more at ease with them than at the tables of the high and the mighty."

At Bombay a small party of Indians boarded the vessel. Wilson, who liked to study people, felt himself strangely attracted to them; though at first he could not fit them into any sort of category. They were poorly but neatly dressed, were very quiet and reserved, and their mannerisms were so correct as to give them an air of studied aloofness. Wilson observed them quietly and they, well aware of his interest, observed him.

It was a sturdy, rather good-looking man they saw; a powerfully built man with tousled hair and a determined jaw. The independent air of his childhood photographs had grown more pronounced; but now the burdens of the world seemed for some reason to have descended on to his broad shoulders. Perhaps he realized that he had, as yet, no purpose in his life.

Wilson met the Indians several times during the last stages of the voyage to England, and he learned that they were Yogis. At first he showed only a polite and rather remote interest in their philosophy of self-discipline and self-denial; but as the weeks passed and he talked to them fairly frequently he became more and more interested in their explanations of a cult which enabled men to endure extreme physical ordeals without ill-effect. But his native shrewdness and common sense were far too deeply ingrained for him to become a practising Yogi!

When the vessel docked at Southampton, Wilson said good-bye to his Indian acquaintances who had, with their talk of Oriental mysticism, helped him to while away the time; they never met again; and as Wilson made his way to London the theories and ideals the Yogis had expounded slipped for the moment from his mind.

Back in London he hoped to start life anew   He had no definite plans; but he had, in his decade of wanderings, set aside enough money to live in reasonable comfort while he looked around. He knew a good many people in the capital, but none of them with any intimacy—he was not a man who formed intimate friendships either lightly or easily. Yet within a few days of his landing he had met and become firm friends with two people who were to play a vital role in the approaching climax of his life.

*   *   *

Enid and Leonard Evans were a young happily married couple in love with each other and with life. Wilson met Leonard Evans quite by chance; he was thinking of buying a car and had been given his name as a reliable dealer. They soon got talking about things other than gear ratios and front suspension, and Evans invited Wilson home to his house in Maida Vale. There he introduced him to his attractive young wife, whose vivacious personality made a lasting impression on Wilson who had up to now been something of a misogynist. The three struck up one of those rare and happy friendships that are all the deeper for the fact that the friends have apparently so little in common. It is enough to say that in this case the three people got to know and understand one another perfectly; friendship such as theirs defies analysis.

Naturally enough, soon after he had taken rooms on the outskirts of London, Wilson went north to Bradford. His father had died a year or two before, his mother was an invalid, and his brothers were carving out successful careers in the textile industry. His family were overjoyed to see him back; but he found that he now had little in common with them. They begged him to return to the industry he had been apprenticed to fifteen years before.

"Why not settle down now, and use your brains?" his mother asked him.

Wilson returned to London with her words pricking at his conscience. He began to wonder not for the first time why he hadn't taken her advice. He asked himself if he really knew what he was looking for in life? Would he even recognize the perfection he longed for if he was lucky enough to find it? Was he chasing a chimera? He took his troubles to his new-found friends; but neither Leonard nor Enid could produce, like a conjuror out of a hat, the touchstone to happiness. However they could, and did offer their friendship and advice. "A trouble shared is a trouble halved," is less trite a saying than it sounds; and there seems little doubt that during the ensuing months this friendship saved

Wilson from a complete nervous breakdown. For soon the house in Maida Vale became a second home to him; often they would sit talking late into the night, and the Evanses came at last to regard Wilson almost as they would a well-loved brother.

But about three months after his return from New Zealand Wilson's health began suddenly to deteriorate. He lost weight and developed a racking cough. His visits to Maida Vale became less and less frequent. Then suddenly he disappeared, leaving only the short cryptic note: "I must shake this thing off. If I come back you'll know that I am all right. If you don't see me again you'll know that I am dead." This was the first of a long series of notes and statements that Wilson was to make—notes that with their sensational bravado reflect the less attractive side of his complex personality. Naturally enough his message caused great anxiety to his friends; but there was nothing they could do but sit back and await events.

It is in the happenings of the next few weeks that the key to Wilson's life can be found.

He took his troubles not to a doctor but to a certain man—he remains nameless in all Wilson's papers—who lived in a luxurious Mayfair flat. This man had, seventeen years before, been told by every doctor he consulted that he had only three months to live. He refused to accept their opinion, and by subjecting himself to certain unorthodox treatment—treatment as much spiritual as physical—he effected in a couple of months an amazing and complete recovery.

There may, of course have been some quite simple explanation, on medical grounds, of his sudden and spectacular cure; but the man himself regarded his recovery as a miracle, nor in the light of what followed is it easy to say that he was wrong.

For after his escape from death he decided to devote his life and his very considerable fortune, to propagating the treatment that had in his case proved so amazingly effective. Within a few years he had brought about complete cures in over a hundred men and women who suffered from diseases as varied and serious as cancer, arthritis, diabetes, tuberculosis and venereal disease. In several cases his treatment proved effective where doctors had diagnosed a patient as incurable; and many members of the medical profession vouched for the authenticity of what can only be termed his "Miracle Cures".

For his treatment consisted, very simply, of two things only: faith and fasting. It would be easy to dub him a crank and his patients dupes, were it not for the fact that the treatment worked, and he never accepted money.

It was to him that Wilson went—an undeniably sick and unhappy man—in the summer of 1932. And within a couple of months he was well, both physically and mentally.

The man told Wilson exactly what he had done to cure himself, and advised him to follow the same treatment to the letter. He had, he said, fasted for thirty-five days, drinking only small quantities of water; during this fast he had been able to purge himself, both physically and mentally, of all extraneous matter. Then, when he had lain completely weak and helpless and not so far from death, he had simply prayed to God that he might, in the words of the Bible, "be born again of water and of the Spirit". His prayer, he said, was answered. And the fact that he was alive helped to prove his point.

Wilson followed the man's advice implicitly and he too was completely cured.

Had he consulted a doctor, his physical recovery would in all probability have been just as effective—and as things turned out a good deal less costly. For the method of his cure was directly responsible for his death, two years later, on Everest.

Once his fast was over Wilson spent a couple of months recuperating in the Black Forest; here in a little café in Freiburg he came across, quite by chance, an old newspaper cutting of the 1924 Expedition to Mount Everest; and this cutting set him thinking.

CHAPTER TWO

THE MOTIVE

W<small>HY, IT</small> has often been asked, do men climb mountains?
They climb them, as Mallory once said, simply because
they are there. They present an eternal challenge; and
because God so made man that he alone of all created
creatures walks upright and can puzzle over the mystery of
the stars, no challenge will remain unanswered for long.
Mankind's yearning to probe the unknown has ever driven
its more adventurous members along the hazardous path of
exploration. The continents, the oceans, the stars: all in
time will yield their secrets. Weren't they put there to be
striven for?

If a man, then, wants to climb a mountain, no other explanation is in a way needed than the fact that the man is a
man and the mountain is there.

But there is another motive force that has, through the
ages, urged explorers on, and this force is very lucidly ex-
plained by Frank Smythe. In his book, *The Spirit of the
Hills*, he writes: "The force that drives men towards the
summit of the highest hills is the same force that has raised
him above the beasts. He is not put into this world merely
to exist; he is put there to find love and happiness, to express and to create. Some achieve happiness best by seeking
out the wildest and most inaccessible corners of the earth,
and there subjugating their bodies to discomfort and even
peril, in search of an ideal which goes by the simple word
'discovery', discovery not only of physical objects but of
themselves."

This discovery of self has not very often been an originating
force in the history of exploration; but once a man sets his
heart on the attaining of some physical objective, he often
finds that the dangers and disappointments he meets call for

him to banish all frailty and weakness from his make-up, and cause him to draw on reserves of tenacity and courage that he never realized he possessed. So it is that many hitherto ordinary men have, when the necessity arose, realized their full stature and have faced hardship and even death with a serenity that is truly God-like. And only those who have realized themselves fully and have obliterated their own weaknesses can be classed among the very greatest of the world's explorers.

The discovery of the Holy Grail could, according to legend, only be achieved by a man who was himself pure and immaculate, both in body and in mind. So it is, to a lesser degree, with lesser quests.

But as well as these two motives there has been one other, of a more practical nature, that has urged explorers on. This motive was shared by Marco Polo, Columbus and Thor Heyerdahl; it is the desire to prove a theory by practical experiment. Columbus believed that the world was round, and to prove he was right he tried to sail around it. Maurice Wilson too had a certain theory to prove, and to prove it he tried to climb Mount Everest.

Nor should the fact that Wilson's theory sounds—when judged by the yardstick of common sense—more than a little fantastic, lead us to condemn him for trying to prove it. For in doing so he was simply following an age-old tradition of the world's greatest explorers.

To understand what Wilson's theory was, we must go back to the Black Forest, where in the autumn of 1932 he was convalescing after his fast.

His letters and diaries confirm that he felt at this time a new man, both physically and mentally. He had put on two stones within a couple of months, and he had lost his cough and his feeling of depression. He felt, literally, as though he had been born again. He was convinced, rightly or wrongly, that his recovery had been due to Divine help. He had followed his mentor's instructions to the letter; he had fasted for thirty-five days, then prayed to God to make him a new man. And God, it seemed to him, had done exactly that.

Now Wilson, although he was both a perfectionist and an idealist, was also a man possessed of no little shrewdness and common sense. And, like many Yorkshiremen, he was above all a practical man. He had seen others cured by fasting and faith; he had been cured by them himself. Here, it seemed to him was a panacea for all the malaise of the world. Yet he knew very well that it was a panacea which the world would not readily accept. It was too unorthodox. He could proclaim his new-found faith in the press, from a pulpit, or from a soap-box, and the world would dub him a crank. The only chance of making people listen to him was to give them some striking and sensational demonstration of the practical effectiveness of his beliefs.

It was while his mind was thinking along these lines that he saw, in the Freiburg café, a cutting about the 1924 Expedition to Everest. He read of the Sherpas and yaks that had carried the elaborate train of equipment to the base of the mountain; he read of the dangers and apparently insurmountable difficulties that had faced the mountaineers. And he asked himself did he truly believe that fasting and Divine faith could accomplish *anything*? No sooner had he asked himself, than he knew his belief was indeed pure and absolute. And he realized what he must do.

He returned to England, and at once got in touch with Enid and Leonard Evans. They were delighted to see him and realized at once that he was now restored to health and also to happiness. They celebrated his homecoming with dinner at a Mayfair restaurant and then went on to a night club. It was in the early hours of the morning that they returned to Maida Vale, but none of them felt tired. Wilson indeed seemed keyed-up with a barely suppressed excitement, and his excitement communicated itself to his friends. It was on this morning at 4 a.m. that Wilson first put forward in concise unmistakable words, the tragic and fantastic theory he was to give his life to prove.

The Evanses listened in silence as he talked until it was

dawn; at first they were sceptical, then they were moved, and finally they were appalled.

"I fasted," Wilson told them "and I prayed and I was made whole. What happened to me can happen to others. My belief is this: If a man fasts—and fasts properly—he at last reaches a stage when his physical body and his soul are one, and he lies close to death but completely drained of all bodily and spiritual ill. Then he is ready to be born again. His body he brings back to life with food. His soul he commits into God's good care, and his soul like his body is born again."

Enid and Leonard Evans looked at Wilson, then doubtfully at one another. Leonard knocked out the ashes from his pipe.

"Sounds a bit far-fetched to me," he said. "Let's have some tea, Enid. You don't catch me fasting for thirty-five days!"

"All right," said Wilson quietly, "forget the fasting if you like: that's only the means and not the end. That leaves us with faith—only faith: the thing that moves mountains, you know. Now I believe that if a man has sufficient faith he can accomplish *anything*. I haven't gone mad, and I haven't got religious mania. But I've got a theory to prove and I intend to try and prove it. I'll show the world what faith can do! I'll perform some task so hard and so exacting that it could only be carried out by someone aided with Divine help. Then if I'm successful perhaps the world will listen to me."

"And what," asked Enid, "are you going to do?"

Wilson pulled a newspaper cutting out of his wallet.

"Look at this," he said. "The 1924 Expedition to Everest. They had three hundred porters, several hundred ponies and a few score yaks. And they didn't get very far, did they? All you need to climb a mountain is a tent, a sleeping bag, warm clothing, food and faith. Now can you guess what I'm going to do?"

The Evanses looked at him in fascinated horror. Maurice Wilson stood up.

"That's right," he said very quietly, "I'll climb Mount Everest alone."

CHAPTER THREE

THE MOUNTAIN

It was a fantastic idea, and in it were all the elements of tragedy. For Everest could not be climbed, by any man, alone; yet it was not in Wilson's nature ever to give up. The end of the venture was, from its very beginning, inevitable.

But he set about his task with optimism and a fair amount of common sense. His first need, he realized, was to find out all he could about the mountain he was challenging; and in the next couple of months he borrowed and studied every book and map on Everest that the London libraries could lend him.

There has in the last few years been such a spate of books about the Himalaya—and Everest in particular—that it is difficult for us to realize how little was known about the mountain in 1933. Even so one might have thought that a careful study of the existing information would have shown Wilson his task was utterly impossible. For already the mountain had taken terrible toll of those who had challenged her. Yet perhaps the very difficulty of his self-appointed task spurred Wilson on. If only he could achieve the impossible then surely the world would listen to him.

It was a fascinating story he gradually pieced together from the books that began to pile up in his "digs" near Maida Vale, and soon he had in his mind a complete picture of Mount Everest and its history.

He read first how the highest mountain in the world was discovered.

He learned that in 1849 the Indian Trigonometrical Survey started to take, from the plains of India, a series of observations on the Nepalese peaks. These often had Indian names, but they were so numerous and thronged and towered so closely together, that some mountains were nameless even to the Indians and Nepalese. These were therefore distinguished by numbers, and among these nameless peaks was one listed simply as Peak XV. It was three years later that a Bengali computer, working out a series of calculations, suddenly realized for the first time the true height of Peak XV. He rushed into the office of the Surveyor-General, Sir Andrew Waugh.

"Sir," he cried, "I've discovered the highest mountain in the world!"

After careful checks had been made it was established that Peak XV was over 29,000 feet high—29,002 was the exact mean height arrived at—and it was decided to name it after Sir George Everest who, as Waugh's predecessor, had set in motion the machinery of the Trigonometrical Survey. Only later did the Everest expeditions discover, when they pushed into the heart of Tibet, that the mountain had in fact a native name—Chomolungma: Goddess Mother of the World.

But though the highest peak was discovered as long ago as 1852, it was many years before it was explored. For Everest rose on the borders of Nepal and Tibet, and both countries denied foreigners permission even to approach the mountain. How the Himalayan peaks were reconnoitred and their rough positions plotted is one of the greatest untold sagas in the history of exploration.

It was impossible for any white man to enter Tibet: the few who tried were quickly and inevitably captured, tortured and returned to India in a condition terrible enough to discourage others from following in their steps. But in 1860 an officer of the Indian Survey, Captain Montgomery, hit on the idea of training a number of intelligent Indians in the use of scientific instruments, and then using them as explorers. These men, known as the "Pundit Explorers" were specially instructed in the technique of making route traverses by compass bearings and the pacing of steps; then, travelling in disguise, they set off into the vast 2,000-mile belt of the unknown Himalaya. Often they were away for years before returning with the precious geographical knowledge that they had, with such danger and physical hardship, so laboriously collected. Every step they took they recorded by the revolution of their prayer-wheels or by the beads on their rosaries; then at night they would write up their notes on tiny rolls of paper which they hid inside the prayer wheels. They recorded compass bearings of the mountains and rivers they passed by using miniature compasses cleverly disguised as amulets. Inside their hollow walking sticks they carried boiling-point thermometers to measure the altitudes. Most of these men whose incredible labours earned them only a few rupees a month, went disguised as pilgrims, priests, or traders. And the danger and hardships they endured were so phenomenal that no single man could accomplish more than two, or at the most three, journeys in his lifetime.

The "Pundits" were indeed brave men, and for nearly half a century the little that was known about Everest was pieced together from their observations. But none of them ever succeeded in penetrating to within more than fifty miles of the summit; for Everest lies half-hidden behind a covering wall of other mountains—great 22,000-foot peaks— which, until they are passed, look higher than the most distant summit. No Pundit ever found his way to Everest's great glacial valleys, though two of them brought back vague rumours of Chamalung—"the Sanctuary of the Birds", and of an age-old "Lamasery of the Snows" whose priests were said to keep watch over the Goddess Mother of the World.

The actual opening up of the approaches to Everest came as a result of Sir Francis Younghusband's military mission to Lhasa. This was in 1904; and one of the concessions extracted from the Dalai Lama was that occasional British expeditions should be allowed to explore and climb in the Tibetan Himalaya.

In the next decade a number of tentative explorations were made. Rawling and Ryder surveyed the Tsampo Valley in the upper reaches of the Brahmaputra. Dr. Kellas patiently plotted a first tentative route from Darjeeling, along the Terta Valley; and he too began the training of Sherpa porters. Then in 1913 Captain John Noel, a young army officer, entered Tibet on an unauthorized journey, and disguised as a native penetrated to within forty miles of Everest.

Wilson may not have paid special attention to Noel's journey when he first read it, but later, when forced to adopt similar methods himself, he doubtless recalled many of its details.

Then in 1914 the Great War put a temporary stop to the exploration of Everest.

In 1919 Sir Charles Bell, the British envoy to Lhasa, obtained permission for two exploratory and climbing expeditions to approach Everest in 1921 and 1922; and the same year the Royal Geographical Society and the Alpine Club combined forces to form the Mount Everest Committee. The fight was on. And soon out of ignorance came knowledge; out of darkness, light.

For early in 1921 there assembled at Darjeeling a reconnaissance expedition under the leadership of Lieut.-Colonel Howard-Bury. And this first expedition was perhaps the most outstandingly successful of all those that ever came to the Himalaya. For not only did it find the way to Everest, it reconnoitred a possible route to the very summit.

The expedition assembled at Darjeeling in early May. The direct route is impossible to follow, being barred by Kangchenjunga and its subsidiary peaks and ranges, and the expedition were soon to find themselves journeying some 300 miles, threading their way slowly through the vast passes and gorges of the Eastern Himalaya, before they reached even the foot of their objective.

On May 18th the great caravan of explorers, porters and pack-animals were ready for the start.

They headed first through the humid jungle and deep valleys of tropical Sikkim, then up and along the broad Chumbi Valley toward the wilderness of the high Tibetan plateau. At first their route was obvious, but after some hundred miles the valley petered out and they had to blaze a trail across the little-known plateau. Their first and most distressing setback was the illness of Dr. Kellas, the expedition's recorder-in-command. Day after day he grew gradually weaker, until as they were crossing a 17,000-foot pass near Kampa Dzong, his heart failed him and he passed quietly away. The following afternoon they saw Everest for the first time, and Kellas was buried within sight of the mountain he had so longed to set foot on.

A couple of days later Harold Raeburn also became ill, and he and Wollaston returned to the lower reaches of the valley. The loss of two members of the climbing party was a serious blow to the expedition, and the task of probing Everest's defences fell almost entirely on the shoulders of Bullock and young Leigh-Mallory. They rose to the occasion magnificently.

The party, after following many a false lead, worked their way gradually to within sixty miles of the north-east face of Everest. Then across the windswept plateau they suddenly had the first real glimpse of the mountain that any European had yet been vouchsafed. It is only fitting that George Leigh-Mallory should describe so great a moment: "We were now able," he writes, "to make out almost exactly where Everest should be; but the clouds were dark in that direction. We gazed at them intently through fieldglasses, as though by some miracle we might pierce the veil. Presently the miracle happened. We caught the gleam of snow behind the grey mists. A whole group of mountains began to appear in gigantic fragments. Mountain shapes are often fantastic seen through a mist, these were like the wildest creation of a dream. A preposterous triangular lump rose out of the depths; its edge came leaping up at an angle of about seventy degrees and ended nowhere. To the left a black, serrated crest was hanging in the sky incredibly. Gradually, very gradually, we saw the great mountain, sides and glaciers and aretes, now one fragment and now another through the

Maurice Wilson . . . the airman

Wilson says good-bye to Enid Evans

floating rifts, until far higher in the sky than imagination had dared to suggest the white summit of Everest appeared."

A week later the expedition pitched camp at the foot of the Rongbuk Valley. They had found "the Lamasery of the Snows" and there ahead of them, displayed in all her majesty and grandeur, lay Everest.

After a few days' reconnaissance Mallory and Bullock formed the conclusion that the only feasible route to the upper slopes was by way of the North Col, a magnificent snow saddle abutting from Everest's north-east ridge to the eastern wall of the Rongbuk Glacier. But their advance to the col along the glacier itself was eventually barred by unscalable precipices, pregnant with avalanche-snow. An alternative route would have to be found, and Mallory rightly thought that an approach along the East Rongbuk Glacier would hold more promise of success. It took the expedition two months to find a way into this glacier—for they missed the narrow defile which links the two Rongbuks together—but after a detour of some hundred miles they finally reached it via the Kharta Valley. Although it was now late September, Morshead and Mallory pushed along the glacier-edge and finally reached the ice-fall guarding the approaches to the North Col.

As Wilson was to learn later—at the cost of his life—the approaches to the North Col are both difficult and hazardous. Steps had to be cut into the glass-like surface of the ice, and the more difficult chimneys carefully roped; but at last Mallory, Bullock, Morshead and Wheeler got through. And men set foot for the first time on Everest's North Col. The key to the mountain had been found, but the weather was too bad for the lock to be turned, and the expedition returned, finding on their way down the narrow link between the two Rongbuk Glaciers.

In four months of adventure and endeavour the secrets of Everest had been at least partially laid bare. Not until September 30th, 1951, when Shipton and Hillary stood on the Pumori Ridge and saw a possible southern route via the

Khumbu Ice Fall and the Lhotse face, was reconnaissance work of equal value carried out on Everest.

As soon as Howard-Bury's reports reached London the Mount Everest Committee set about its work in earnest, and in March, 1922, the first climbing expedition set out from Darjeeling; it was composed of thirteen Britishers, 160 Sherpas and porters, and over three hundred pack animals—almost an army in miniature. Its leader was Brigadier-General Charles Bruce, and among its members were the pick of England's mountaineers—men such as Norton, Somervell, Finch and Mallory.

They followed Howard-Bury's route to Rongbuk, then instead of approaching the North Col via the Kharta Valley, the expedition pushed straight up the Rongbuk Glacier, then cut through the narrow defile into the East Rongbuk. Camps I, II and III were, with some difficulty, established along the length of the glacier, the last being in the basin immediately below the ice-fall. It took them several days to negotiate the fall, but eventually they set up Camp IV at some 23,000 feet. Then their troubles began.

Immediately above the ice fall lay 2,000 feet of comparatively easy climbing. But the cold was intense, the lack of oxygen brought about a feeling of extreme lassitude, and above Camp V—at 25,000 feet—the climbing became, once again, extremely difficult. That first night at Camp V all four men—Mallory, Morshead, Somervell and Norton—were frost-bitten. Mallory's finger tips became dead white and lost all feeling; Morshead suffered from intense sickness as well as frost-bite on fingers and toes; Somervell was perhaps in the best shape though his throat was very painful, and Norton's left ear was frost-bitten so badly that he could that night lie only on one side. Morshead, it soon became apparent, was very seriously ill, and rather than hamper the others he decided to make his way down to Camp IV alone. Mallory, Somervell and Norton went on to reach a height of nearly 27,000 feet, before, suffering agonies from lassitude, lack of oxygen and almost unbelievable cold they retreated to safety, picking up Morshead at Camp IV. This return down the ice fall, with Morshead too ill to help himself, was an epic of endurance and mountaineering skill. Three days later another assault party—Finch, Bruce and Tejbir—set off for the summit. A murderous storm kept them snow-bound at Camp V for two days, expecting at any moment they would be blown some 8,000 feet down the mountain on to the glaciers far below. Then they crept on, only for Tejbir to collapse at 26,000 feet and later struggle back alone. Finch and Bruce eventually reached 27,300 feet before being forced back. "Though some 1,700 feet below, we were within half a mile of the summit," wrote Finch; "so close indeed that we could distinguish individual stones on a little patch of scree lying just underneath the highest point. Ours were truly the tortures of Tantalus; for weak with hunger and exhausted by the nightmare struggle for life, we were in no fit condition to proceed. Indeed I knew that if we were to persist in climbing even only another 500 feet we should not get back alive."

The climbers retired for a fortnight to the Base Camp, which soon began to take on the appearance of a field hos-pital; then it was decided that Mallory and Somervell should launch a final assault. It was while they and their porters were climbing the deceptively steep slopes of the ice fall that an avalanche swept down on them, and seven men lost their lives. Further progress was out of the question, and saddened by the loss of seven of their porters the party returned to Darjeeling. The seven Sherpas could have had no finer epitaph than the words of Mallory who wrote, "Everest is beyond the range of a simple contract measured in terms of money: the porters had come to have a share in our enterprise, and these men died in an act of voluntary service freely rendered and faithfully performed."

From the accounts he read of these expeditions Wilson should have learned two lessons. Firstly that a possible way to the summit via the East Rongbuk Glacier and the North Col did in fact exist; and secondly that to follow this route was beyond the capabilities of any single man, even a highly-skilled mountaineer. But of the two lessons he learned only the first. Nor did the tragedy of the following expedition—that of 1924—appear to drive home the point that if the summit of Everest was beyond the reach of a party of highly-skilled mountaineers, it was also beyond the reach of a lone inexpert climber—no matter how great his courage, no matter how immovable his faith.

For from the assault of 1924 there stemmed the most moving and imperishable chapter in the history of mountaineering: the deaths of George Leigh-Mallory and Andrew Irvine.

This expedition, led by General Bruce, set out on a high note of confidence. It could benefit from the lessons learned in 1922; also among its members were four men—Mallory, Somervell, Bruce and Norton—who had at that time climbed higher than any others in the world.

They left Darjeeling on March 25th and arrived in the Rongbuk valley some five weeks later. They were met with the most appalling weather. In a full gale, with incredibly low temperatures and squalls of blinding snow, a string of camps were painfully established along the floor of the East Rongbuk Glacier. But the weather was too bad for them to be held, and sadly depleted by illness and injury among the Sherpas, the party retired to their Base Camp.

At the first hint of better weather the glacier was climbed again, and by May 19th, Camp III was re-established below the ice fall guarding the approaches to the North Col. The scaling of this precipitous wall of serrated ice and unstable snow proved a difficult task, but eventually Camp IV was pitched on the col, only for it to be evacuated a few days later because of appalling weather. Four porters were marooned above the ice fall—all of them frostbitten and with very little food—and on May 24th, Norton, Somervell and Mallory set out to bring them down. They had an exhausting and nerve-racking day. The ice fall was blanketed in soft, feathery snow. The Sherpas were in bad shape and had to be helped down—once two of them set off an avalanche which almost precipitated them over a 200-foot cliff of ice; they had to fight all the way against bad weather, utter exhaustion and the approaching darkness. It was 7.30 p.m. before, by the light of Norton's torch, they saw Noel and Odell coming to meet them a little above Camp III. Frostbite, lassitude and snow blindness again took their toll of both Britishers and Sherpas, and once more the expedition retired to the Base Camp.

Rest at lower altitudes was badly needed; yet in a very few days the monsoon would come sweeping up from the south. The situation could hardly have been more depressing; for they had planned to be established on the north-west arete by mid-May, yet it was now almost June and they had hardly set foot on the upper slopes. It was clear they must strike hard and fast or else admit defeat.

At the very end of May the weather again cleared and three assaults were launched, one after another, on the summit. The last two were epics in the history of mountaineering.

The first assault was by Mallory and Geoffrey Bruce. With Irvine, Odell and nine porters they reached the North Col in three days and spent the night there. Next morning leaving Odell and Irvine and one porter in support, they struck up along the north-east ridge accompanied by the eight remaining "Tigers". They made good progress that first day and established Camp V at 25,000 feet. Then the weather deteriorated. In a night of bitter cold and shrieking wind none of them slept for more than a couple of hours; and next morning the porters refused to go higher. Nor would Bruce's eloquence or Mallory's singleness of purpose induce them to climb another step. Bitterly disappointed the first assault party returned to the North Col.

Meanwhile Norton and Somervell, the second assault party, were working their way up the mountain one day behind the others.

On June 2nd together with six porters they left Camp IV and struck out along the western tip of the col. At first, in a shallow tunnel, they were exposed to the full force of the biting wind, then they emerged into sunlight as they progressed slowly along the blunt ridge of the north-east arete. The wind was cutting and the slopes deceptively steep; but at least the sun brought them a little warmth and the climbing was not technically difficult. Soon they met the first party despondently descending; then they reached Camp V, a little after 1 p.m. Though it was early they decided to conserve their energy for the next day and settle down for an early night.

Norton's diary records that they spent a "fair night", which at over 25,000 feet is about the best that can be hoped for; and at 9 a.m.—four hours after they had got up—they were off again. This day too they made fair progress. The Sherpas were remarkably cheerful, though they could move only very slowly; the weather was fine; and soon they passed the highest spot reached by the expedition of 1922. Norton and Somervell sent the porters down at about one-thirty and settled down to a lonely night in a shelving cleft in the rock at some 26,800 feet.

Although their tent was pitched on a steep slope—Norton writes that, "in the whole north arete of Everest I have never seen a single spot affording the six-foot square area on which a tent could be pitched without having first to build a platform . . ."—they again spent a fair night. Norton indeed, in spite of finding next morning that his cold thermos flask had emptied itself into his bed, spent the best night since leaving Camp V, while Somervell, though he did not sleep too well, was at least fairly comfortable.

They must that night have dreamed of success.

Next day they got off to an early start, and 7 a.m. saw them making good progress, traversing diagonally across a series of broad, comparatively easy ledges. But gradually the effects of altitude became more pronounced. They were higher now than any man had stood before, and Somervell's throat and cough were causing him great pain and exhaustion, while Norton was experiencing trouble with his eyes:

"I was seeing double," he later wrote, "and in a difficult step was sometimes in doubt where to put my feet." Their pace became slower and slower. Soon they could manage less than a dozen steps at a time; and every five or ten minutes they rested panting and coughing for breath.

Towards noon they found themselves nearing the great couloir which slashes down between the final pyramid and the great northern shoulder. Here Somervell succumbed to his throat trouble. He told Norton he was only hindering him, and urged him to try alone for the summit—now only some 1,000 feet above them.

For a little over an hour Norton pushed on alone, working his way parallel to and some 500 feet below the crest of the north-east arete. As he approached the great couloir he met a covering of fine powder snow which concealed the unstable footholds. The angle of the slope increased, and beyond the couloir the going became difficult and extremely dangerous: a single slip would have hurtled him some 8,000 feet on to the upper reaches of the main Rongbuk Glacier. In an hour Norton gained only some hundred feet; there were still another 800 to go and he realized it would be quite impossible for him to reach the summit and return alive.

Slowly and painfully he retraced his steps; then together with Somervell made his way back to safety. They reached Camp IV long after dark, and the next day Norton found himself completely snow-blind and in great pain. For three days he was quite unable to see; and how much he suffered in those long hours of pain and darkness no man will ever know. But he had climbed to 28,126 feet.

The third attempt was to cost the lives of George Leigh-Mallory and Andrew Irvine.

A great deal has been written about their last tragic climb; tens of thousands of words have been poured out in an attempt to prove either they did or did not reach the summit. This is not the place even to summarize the vast and conflicting mass of evidence. And the question is, in any case, largely irrelevant. Does it make Mallory and Irvine any the nobler if they fell on the way down rather than the way up? As Mallory had himself written after the successful accomplishment of a previous climb. "Have we achieved success? That word means nothing here. . . ."

At eight-forty on the morning of June 6th, Mallory and Irvine set out from Camp IV. They had breakfasted on fried sardines, biscuits, hot tea and chocolate, and each carried a 25 lb. pack. It was a brilliant morning, and they quickly reached Camp V, where Mallory wrote in his diary, "there is no wind here, and things look hopeful". The next day they pushed up to Camp VI, and Odell and the Sherpa Nema followed them to Camp V in support. And the next day they left Camp VI for a final bid for the summit, and Odell, alone, followed them up to the camp they had rested in the night before. It was a little after noon that Odell caught a last glimpse of them, high up on the arete. He wrote later: "There was a sudden clearing of the atmosphere above me and I saw the whole summit ridge and the final peak of Everest unveiled. I noticed far away on a snow slope, leading up to what seemed to me to be the last step but one from the base of the final pyramid, a tiny object moving and approaching the rock step. A second object followed, and then the first climbed to the top of the step. As I stood intently watching this dramatic appearance, the scene became enveloped in cloud once more and I could not actually be certain that I saw the second figure join the first."

Mallory and Irvine were never seen again.

Odell did not spare himself when the next morning they failed to return. Alone, he twice climbed to over 27,000 feet in his determined efforts to find trace of them; but at last, when all hope was gone, he came slowly back. Everest had again taken her toll. And this time one of her victims had been her most persistent challenger—the man who had done more than any other to lay bare her secrets, and whose indomitable spirit had been the driving force behind three great expeditions.

One cannot help but ask why Wilson thought he could

succeed where men such as Mallory had failed. But perhaps
the sincerely held faith of a man should not be judged by
the yardstick of common sense. Such, right or wrong, was
Wilson's belief. He was prepared to die for it. Who are we
to question it?

*   *   *

The accounts of the 1924 expedition were the last Wilson
was to read about an actual attempt to climb Mount Everest.
For eight years were to pass before the Dalai Lama gave
permission for another expedition to pass through Tibet. He
and his advisers deplored the disasters and the loss of life
that had taken place in 1922 and 1924, and they returned to
their traditional policy of isolation from the rest of the world.

But in 1932, at about the time Wilson first conceived his
own fantastic plan, the Dalai Lama gave way before the
friendly pressure brought to bear on him by the India Office
and the British Political Agent in Sikkim, and gave permission for a fourth expedition to Everest. At once preparations were set under way to enable a party of British
climbers to leave England early in 1933 under the leadership
of Hugh Ruttledge. This party did in fact attempt Mount
Everest the year before Wilson; but he never saw their reports or spoke to any of the members.

Such was the scanty and incomplete information on
Everest available to Wilson when he made his plans. There
was, however, one other factor which possibly he took into
account; and this was the never-ending literature and correspondence about the ideal size of a mountaineering expedition. This correspondence had not yet reached its climax,
but the question nevertheless was one that was perennially
raised in the press, books and journals, and Wilson doubtless
thought that if the experts themselves could not agree
whether two or two hundred was the better size for an expedition, there was no reason why he should not advocate
and put into practice an expedition of one.

There are two very decided schools of thought as to what

constitutes an ideal climbing party in the Himalaya. There are, on the one hand, those who feel that the highest peaks in the world present such extreme difficulty that they can only be overcome by a large expedition, an expedition that plans its assault with all the care and marshalling of resources of a war-time offensive. In the view of these men the end—the successful attaining of a summit—justifies the means. Such was the belief of Mallory, Ruttledge and Sir John Hunt.

On the other hand there are those who feel that large expeditions are inherently inefficient and also harmful to the best interests of mountaineering. It is felt by this school of thought that small expeditions are easier, pleasanter, and just as likely to achieve their objective, also they avoid the attendant fuss, sensationalism and limelight that is naturally focused on a large party which has, of necessity, been at least partially financed by the Press—who naturally enough expect a *quid pro quo* for their money in the shape of some exciting headlines. In the view of these men mountaineering is a sport and a way of life and not an all-out military offensive. Such was the belief of Sir Francis Younghusband, Tilman and Eric Shipton.

It is obvious that the beliefs of this second school—whose members were essentially individualists—should attract Wilson. And it is surely true that of the two theirs is the nobler conception of mountaineering. Nor is it the less successful. For though it was Sir John Hunt with his large-scale expedition who actually climbed Mount Everest, it was Eric Shipton, with his small parties of the early 1950s, who found and reconnoitred the way.

But comparisons are odious, and in any case mountaineering is something large enough to embrace both schools of thought.

We can imagine Wilson, as gradually his reading made him at least a vicarious Everester, aligning himself on the side of the individualists, and carrying their beliefs to their logical extreme. "If an expedition of three men, why not of two? If of two men, why not of one?"

Eric Shipton was, soon after Wilson's death, to give his own views on this question. "Opinions vary considerably," he wrote, "regarding the optimum size of expeditions. I once asked my friend Dr. Humphreys for his views on the matter. He replied firmly and without hesitation, 'three constitutes a large expedition, and a party of one may be considered a small expedition.' I do not propose anything so drastic for an attempt on Mount Everest, though I have always thought that a party of three climbers would stand almost as good a chance as any larger number. . . . For my part I loathed the crowds and the fuss that were inseparable from a large expedition. I always had the ridiculous feeling that I was taking part in a Cooks' tour or a school treat, and I wanted to go away and hide myself."

Though Shipton wrote this after Wilson's death, very similar opinions were expressed in the early 1930s when the latter was planning his lone assault. But Wilson seems to have taken no account of the fact that not a single Everester, not a single mountaineer who had climbed in the Himalaya, not indeed a single mountaineer of any standing or experience would for a moment have condoned a lone assault on such a mountain as this. Any Everester could have told Wilson that on the slopes of The Goddess Mother of the World the difference between one and three is far, far greater than the difference between three and three hundred. But this vital and fundamental point Wilson failed to grasp.

He also failed to appreciate one other point: the technical climbing difficulties which the ascent of Everest presented.

It is a well-known fact that mountaineers are usually modest and reticent men; men who prefer understatement to overstatement, and who minimize rather than exaggerate the difficulties they have to face. As a result of this, there is, in the early literature on Everest, comparatively little mention of the technical climbing difficulties that were met with. And this is for two reasons: firstly the reticence already mentioned; and secondly the fact that only in two places does the north face of Everest present to the highly skilled

mountaineers technical problems which compare in difficulty with the many other problems that have to be faced—
especially bad weather and the difficulty in breathing at a
high altitude.

The two places that did present some difficulty were the
ice-fall guarding the approaches to North Col, and the last
1,500 feet of the final pyramid. And there seems little
doubt that Wilson sadly under-estimated the technical
difficulty of these two stretches.

Yet it is this very miscalculation which in a way adds a
grandeur to the tragedy of his story. For when, among the
seracs and pinnacles of the ice-fall, he must surely have come
at last to realize that his task was utterly beyond him, yet he
struggled on. He never gave up. He was the pioneer on the
roof of the world :

> "Who dares to climb,
>   Although he fall
> A thousand times;
>   Who dares to crawl
> On bloody hands and knees
> Along its stony ecstasies
> Up to the utmost snows;
> Nor knows
> He stands on these . . .
> Or knowing, does not care
> Save to climb on from there !"

Maurice Wilson may never in the technical sense have
been a mountaineer. But his spirit was that of Mallory and
Irvine.

CHAPTER FOUR

"I'LL FLY ALONE TO INDIA"

By the time he had read the whole of the known literature on Everest, Wilson might well have come to the conclusion that in trying to climb the mountain alone he was attempting the impossible. But a full realization of the dangers and difficulties involved served only to increase his determination. "Nothing," he wrote, "can stop my trying to climb Mount Everest. Obviously I think I can do it, or I shouldn't be going to try."

His first practical problem was how to get within striking distance of his objective. This question Wilson solved in a typically forthright manner. "No strings of Sherpas and yaks for me," he told his friends. "No tiring myself out before I ever get there. How shall I manage it? I'll fly." The fact that he had never been up in an aeroplane before, let alone piloted one, did not seem to worry him!

This decision to fly to Everest sprang in the first instance from his reading a report on the projected Houston Everest Flying Expedition, which in the early spring of 1933 was now being planned and financed by Lady Houston. This expedition consisted of two Westland planes, one of which would be flown by the Marquess of Douglas and Clydesdale and the other by Flight-Lieutenant D. F. McIntyre, R.A.F. It was hoped that men would now be able, for the first time, to look down on the highest peak in the world. This would not of course be a conquest of Everest; but if a plane could safely fly, at high altitude, through the treacherous weather and difficult air conditions of the Himalaya, it would serve to underline recent progress in aviation. It was also expected that the photographs taken during the flight would be of great help to later climbing expeditions.

Wilson's first reaction, on hearing of those projected

flights, was to try and combine forces with the Houston party. He seemed to cherish what can only be described as a sadly crack-brained scheme; namely that he should accompany the expedition to India, and that when the time came for the flight over Everest he should be given a wing lift, should parachute on to the lower slopes of the mountain and thence make his way to the top. It is hard to believe that Wilson seriously contemplated such a crazy venture. It is true that wing lifts were sometimes possible for short periods, on certain types of slow speed aircraft which flew at low altitude; but the idea of a wing lift on a Westland aircraft flying comparatively fast and at over 10,000 feet was quite ridiculous. And a parachute landing on the lower slopes of Everest would have almost certainly resulted in serious injury if not in death. It seems that Wilson in fact only put forward this fantastic notion privately to a few friends and never laid himself open to ridicule by expressing it publicly. But it turned his mind to the whole question of how much of his lone assault on Everest should be made by air. And his friends, when they heard his next proposal, noticed a determined glint in his eyes.

"Suppose," he said, "I fly by myself to Everest, and crashland on the lower slopes. Then it will be a straight, short climb to the top."

His friends pointed out that there were two small points he seemed to have overlooked: he couldn't fly and he couldn't climb.

Wilson smiled patiently. "I know," he said. "But I can learn."

*   *   *

The period between the two world wars forms a romantic era in the history of aviation. For these were the years when men and women unfettered the shackles which had so long bound them to the earth, and pitted their skill, courage and tenacity against a new element which they now challenged for the first time—the air. The decade 1925–35 was perhaps the golden age of aviation; for lone adventurers in these ten years blazed new routes around the globe. Frail machines quested the sky in far-flung corners of the world; many of them crashed in ocean or jungle, or desert or mountain range; but many more reached their destination and names such as Jim Mollison, Jean Batten and Alan Cobham became household words.

Maurice Wilson had never flown before, but having set his heart on travelling to Everest by plane, he entered wholeheartedly into the spirit of men's new-born challenge to the air and quickly became an enthusiastic, if not very skilful pilot. His first step was to buy a plane. He studied the reports of famous flights, he talked to pilots and he visited the factories of the leading aircraft companies. It was only after much careful thought that he decided which type of aircraft would be best suited to his purpose. It was a De Havilland Gipsy Moth that he eventually settled on, a biplane with a 55–100 horsepower engine that had been flown by such famous pilots as Amy Johnson, Cobham and Mollison. He could not easily afford a new machine, so he decided to buy a second-hand one. He was a shrewd enough business man to make a good buy, and after answering several advertisements he finally purchased a 1930 Gipsy Moth, with the serial letters G-ABJC.

It was typical of Wilson that he bought the plane before he had learned to fly; an action which underlined both his determination and his egotistical self-assurance. A week after he took delivery of the Moth Wilson joined the London Aero Club.

The Club in those days had its headquarters at Stag Lane, one of the De Havilland aerodromes near Edgware, Middlesex. Here Wilson housed his plane in a hangar on the airfield perimeter, and here he came, week after week, for his initial flying instruction. But before his lessons had even started he aroused the curiosity of the club members by painting the words "EVER WREST" on the nose of his aircraft. When questioned, he gave a carefully prepared statement. "I intend," he said, "to fly to the lower slopes of

Everest; land there, probably at about 14,000 feet, and then continue on foot. I know I shall be taking a big chance, but I shall pray for a safe landing." The more experienced pilots of the club smiled pityingly; their new member was putting a good deal of faith in his machine, not to mention in his own unproved ability as a pilot.

The Chief Flying Instructor at Stag Lane, Nigel Tangye, had heard a good deal about Wilson, and he decided to take him on as one of his own pupils. One afternoon the Instructor was walking with a colleague across the tarmac when Wilson hove in sight. Tangye had been warned what to expect, but even so, he and his friend pulled up short in amazement as Wilson strode briskly toward them. He was wearing huge hobnail boots, fawn-coloured breeches tucked in at the calf by high gaiters and a voluminous leather jerkin. Tangye eyed him askance.

"Who's that fellow?" muttered his friend. "Ask him if he wants the riding stables!"

"That, I am afraid," said Tangye, "is my new pupil."

It was hardly an auspicious start; but none the less there quickly developed between instructor and pupil a very real friendship. Tangye realized, however, from their earliest flight together, that Wilson would never make a good pilot. Of all the qualities needed to fly a plane it soon became obvious to Tangye that his eccentric pupil possessed only two: courage and determination. Even during the first lesson Tangye could see that Wilson was going to be a problem child.

"No! No! No!" he cried. "Don't be so violent, man! Make your movements slowly and smoothly. Not like a butcher hacking up the scrag-end!"

Day after day, week after week, the same heartfelt plea rose into the sky above Stag Lane, as Wilson hurtled the unfortunate Tangye around the winter sky. Wilson's flying instructions proved nerve-racking for the Instructor and costly for the pupil. While under training embryo pilots were usually charged thirty shillings an hour for instruc-

Godspeed . . . from Jean Batten, the famous airwoman

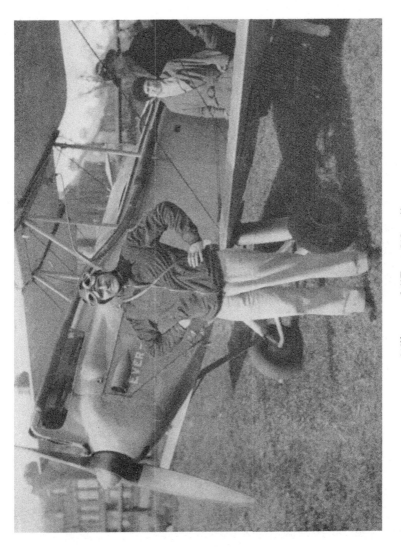

Wilson and "Ever Wrest"

tional flights in the Club's dual-control, two-seater Moth. The cost for a pilot to qualify for his "A" Certificate generally worked out at a little under £20; for to gain this Certificate a pilot had only to complete three hours' solo flying, and an average pupil was ready to fly solo after eight or ten one-hour sessions. But Wilson flew with Tangye for more than nineteen hours before the latter could trust his pupil to take up a plane alone. And even so, the first take-off and landing was a sorry affair, the plane first swinging out of wind and then coming down with a series of frog-like bounces.

"You want to fly to India," said Tangye, as ten minutes later they walked away from the hangars, "but you'll never do it unless you learn to handle your plane more gently."

Wilson's lips tightened. "I'll manage," he said. "I'll fly to India alone or die in the attempt."

That, thought Tangye, was more than probable.

But as the weeks went by and the bond of friendship, based on mutual respect, began to grow between them, Tangye tried his hardest to dissuade Wilson from his attempt on Everest. It was not so much that he disapproved of the idea; he simply thought, with some justification, that Wilson was hardly likely to reach India alive. To fly five thousand miles in an open biplane, over some of the most desolate country of the world, would be an achievement that any experienced pilot might well be proud of. For an inexpert pilot with only a handful of solo flying hours, it seemed a venture that could end only in disaster.

Another man who did his best to make Wilson abandon his project was a certain Major Hemming, the managing director of a company engaged on a scheme of world-wide air survey. Hemming met Wilson several times at the Club. He admired him for his courage and singleness of mind, and offered him a good position in his company.

"Come in with us," he said, "I'll see you get all the adventure you want!"

But it was not adventure that Wilson sought.

The weeks lengthened into months before he got his "A" Certificate. This was a step in the right direction, but it certainly did not mean that he was now an expert or even a competent pilot. This Wilson realized, and he made a determined effort to improve. His solo hours mounted rapidly. He took to arriving at Stag Lane only a little after dawn, and people living near the 'drome breakfasted to the sound of his Gipsy Moth circling erratically overhead.

Tangye made a last effort to dissuade Wilson from his flight, the details of which he was now starting to plan.

"I tell you," the Instructor said, "you're taking on a job that's quite beyond you. Give it up before it's too late."

"That I'll never do!" cried Wilson defiantly, and with a breezy "Cheerio!" he was off across the tarmac, his hobnail boots clattering defiantly.

It was principally with Enid and Leonard Evans that Wilson discussed the details of his approaching flight. While learning to fly he had moved out to Edgware, to "digs" not far from Stag Lane, and from here it was quite a simple journey to Maida Vale. The three of them spent many pleasant evenings in the Evanses' home discussing the route and the equipment that would be needed. Leonard Evans made it clear from the start that he had his doubts about the feasibility of Wilson's lone assault; his wife on the other hand always displayed complete confidence in Wilson's ability to see his mission through. But neither of them, now or at any subsequent stage, ever tried to dissuade him. Those who doubt and trample on their friends' ideals are friends in name alone.

Wilson began to buy equipment for his days on the mountain. And the careful and methodical nature of his purchases showed that his assault was not the hastily-conceived and ill-executed project that some were later to dub it. His tent and sleeping-bag, for example, were of the "improved" type, made specially for the Ruttledge expedition, which incidentally was now on its way to Everest. His clothing was light but warm. Two of his last purchases

were a height recorder, which he said would provide proof
of his ascent, and a light camera. The latter had an auto-
matic shutter which when set would allow him fifteen
seconds to move into the picture. By using this he hoped to
photograph himself standing on the summit. His attitude
towards the use of oxygen was eminently sane. He had read
about the difficulties in breathing experienced by members
of earlier expeditions, and he considered it possible that a
man would not be able to breathe enough of the rarefied air
at 29,000 feet to keep alive. He therefore decided to take
oxygen with him, and had special light-weight equipment
made which weighed under fourteen pounds.

"About oxygen," he wrote, "I simply don't know. I
shan't use it unless I absolutely have to. But I'm taking it
with me in case."

His preparations were by no means confined to flying
lessons and the buying of equipment. He went into strict
training. In his hobnail boots he walked, much to the amuse-
ment of the Club members, round and round the perimeter
of Stag Lane. He was never seen in their Club House.

"I don't need a drink," he told Tangye, "I'm an apple
and nuts man!"

And he did indeed embark on a strict and lengthy diet.

His training consisted in the main of long and vigorous
walks. He walked several times from London to Bradford
in considerably less than five days. He thought nothing of
walking fifteen miles in a single evening. In February he
made a serious effort to learn to climb; but here his preparations fell pathetically short of what was obviously required. He went for five weeks to the Lake District and later
to the Welsh Mountains; but he seems to have made no
serious attempt to acquire even the fundamentals of a mountaineer's basic technique. He spent most of his time on long
hikes, with a little scree scrambling and rock climbing
thrown in. Even the most elementary principles of snow
climbing—such as step cutting and the use of crampons—
were a closed book to him. He did a little rope work, of the

variety used by a lone climber, but as he intended to make his assault alone, ropes, in their generally accepted role of safeguarding the members of a party, were obviously of no use to him.

March saw him back in London, making a few final modifications to his plane.

It was about this time that the Press began to take a serious interest in his approaching flight. On the whole Wilson was well served by the newspapers. He was a man who liked to be interviewed, and he allowed reporters to quote him freely. Soon he became good "copy", and longish articles about him and his fantastic quest began to appear almost daily in the national press. He found a specially strong ally in the *Daily Express*. One newspaper, however, launched a vitriolic attack on what they called his "elaborate suicide". Wilson was furious and told Evans, to whom he had entrusted his affairs, that if he won his battle with Everest this paper should be completely ignored. Photographs of Wilson, always in hobnail boots, leaning nonchalantly against his "Ever Wrest", invariably went side by side with the articles.

And early in April he gave the Press something fresh to write about. Quite by chance he met one evening two reporters, coming out of the tube at Piccadilly. They noticed he was limping, though very slightly.

"What have you been up to?" one of them asked.

"My limp?" said Wilson cheerfully, "I got that when I made my parachute jump."

"When was that?"

Wilson looked at his watch. "Not quite twenty minutes ago."

The reporters looked at each other. "And why," one of them asked, "did you make the jump?"

Wilson smiled. "Just to test my nerve," he said.

And there, as far as he was concerned, the matter ended. But a couple of days later he was warned by the Air Ministry against making unauthorized jumps over London.

The modifications to "Ever Wrest" took longer than

Wilson had bargained for. The first necessity was for a special long-range fuel tank to be fitted into the passenger's cockpit. This was done at the De Havilland workshops. Then Wilson—who at least seemed to have a fair appreciation of his own ability in landing—thought that a heavier and stronger undercarriage ought to be fitted. Tangye wholeheartedly agreed, and "Ever Wrest" paid yet another visit to the De Havilland hangars. But at last the modifications were completed, the plane was thoroughly overhauled, and Wilson settled on a definite date for his departure—Friday, April 21st, his birthday.

He bought a series of large-scale maps covering his proposed route; and these he studied in detail with the Evanses noting the danger areas and marking up the aerodromes at which he hoped to refuel. He planned to fly by a reasonably direct route. His first touch-down would be at Freiburg where he reckoned to spend the week-end with friends. His next call would be at a small aerodrome near Passau on the border of the Austrian Tyrol, where he would refuel before his flight across the Alps. This part of his route he mapped out with special care—for several planes had recently crashed while attempting the crossing—and he worked out a series of tracks which would enable him to give the higher peaks a wide berth; having no oxygen he restricted himself to flying at well under 10,000 feet. Once the Alps were left behind he routed "Ever Wrest" in easy stages down the West Italian coast, landing at Milan, Rome, Naples and Palermo. Italy in late April or early May seemed to promise, after the cold and fog of Stag Lane, a prospect of paradise.

After Palermo, Tunis. He laid his track along the shortest possible sea crossing of the Mediterranean, from Marsala to Cape Bon, and then he singled out for his refuelling the desert air-strips that were ten years later to become famous in the North African Campaign—Tripoli, Benghazi, Tobruk and Sidi Barrani. This part of his flight lay largely over desert wastes, where a forced landing would leave him little chance of survival; but he took what precautions he could by making up what he called a "life-saving pack" built around a first-aid kit and three unbreakable flasks of water. His second week-end he planned to spend in either Alexandria or Cairo, where he hoped to pick up permits for the next stage of his flight, across Arabia to Baghdad, thence, skirting the north coast of the Persian Gulf, into Baluchistan.

Once in India he planned to follow the River Indus north-eastward into the Punjab, then cut across to the Ganges and follow the latter to Purnea.

It was a flight of some 5,000 miles, much of it over difficult terrain. Only a couple of years earlier Jean Batten had followed much the same route in her pioneer flight to Australia—and her flight had very rightly been acclaimed as a magnificent achievement. Obviously Wilson's proposed flight, in a light open aircraft, was one which would have taxed the skill and endurance of the most experienced pilot. For a man with less than two hundred hours of solo flying it seemed a highly dangerous and almost impossible venture.

"How long do you plan to take over the flight," Wilson was asked.

"Only a fortnight," he replied. "That'll be more than enough."

Mid-April saw him about to fly north to bid good-bye to his family; but he suddenly went down with tonsilitis. This was a sad blow to his plans; for he had hoped to reach Everest early in May and make his assault at once, before the monsoon broke at the end of the month. It looked now as though his attempt might have to be postponed for a whole year. Wilson, however, fasted and prayed and at the end of a week declared himself perfectly fit. On Sunday, April 23rd, he made final plans for his departure the next day, and that morning took off from Stag Lane to fly to Bradford where his family were waiting for him to say good-bye.

It was during this flight, on the very eve of his departure, that the inevitable happened.

When "Ever Wrest" took off late that Sunday morning from the aerodrome at Stag Lane, her four-cylinder engine seemed to be running well; but at three in the afternoon as the plane was approaching Brighouse, only a few miles from his destination, it began to cough and splutter. Wilson tried to gain height, but—typically—jerked the stick back too roughly and the plane stalled. "Ever Wrest" spun helplessly toward the Yorkshire moors. By the time Wilson had brought her under control she was flying at less than 800 feet; then the engine stopped coughing and cut out completely. Wilson searched the moors anxiously for a place to try a forced-landing. As luck would have it a large field, with only a handful of cattle in it, was almost directly below him, and Wilson circled this as "Ever Wrest" rapidly lost height. His attempt at a forced-landing would have made Tangye's hair stand on end! Wilson miscalculated almost everything, and came in cross wind, and undershot the field by a good fifty yards. The wheels of "Ever Wrest" tore through a hedge, the plane cartwheeled over, and ended up on its nose in a small country lane.

Wilson was lucky not to be killed; but as chance would have it he was not even scratched, and simply hung there upside-down suspended from his safety-harness, while he mentally assessed the damage to his plane. There he was found by a small boy who jumped off his bicycle and asked politely.

"Can I help you down, mister?"

He undid the safety belt and Wilson tumbled to the ground. He was still ruefully inspecting the damage when ten minutes later a Press photographer arrived and the newspapers next morning were full of pictures of Maurice Wilson standing, with apparent pride, beside his crashed plane.

That night "Ever Wrest" was hoisted on to a lorry and taken the two hundred miles to London; she was in the De Havilland repair shop by 7 a.m. the next day. Here the patient and long-suffering Tangye inspected the damage, which was considerable. It would take at least three weeks, he said, to make her airworthy.

Wilson was bitterly disappointed, for this delay meant the almost certain postponement of his plans. But he decided to leave for India as soon as the plane was ready. Even though he might not be able to climb Everest that year at least he would be on the spot and could do some useful reconnaissance.

In the meanwhile the two Westland planes of the Houston Air Expedition had flown over Everest; and the land expedition led by Hugh Ruttledge had established its base camp. Wilson watched anxiously as the assault on the mountain reached its climax. It would steal much of his thunder if Ruttledge met with success. But, judging by the reports that came through, Ruttledge was progressing only very slowly in the face of appalling difficulties.

At last "Ever Wrest" was ready, and a new departure date was fixed: Sunday, May 21st.

Somewhat belated efforts to stop the flight were made at the last minute by the Air Ministry. Their first letter reached Wilson on May 9th, and read:

"Sir,
I am directed to refer to your proposed flight to Purnea, N.E. India and return in de Havilland Moth aeroplane G-ABJC.

In this connection, I am to inquire whether the recent reports which have appeared in the Press, viz., that after arrival at Purnea you propose to fly to and land upon the slopes of Mount Everest, have any foundation.

I am to point out that the previous permission of the Government of Nepal is required for flight over their territory and you could not be permitted to fly from Purnea across the frontier into Nepal unless such permission had been obtained. The Air Ministry consider it unlikely that the Nepalese Government would grant permission for you to fly over their territory to Mount Everest.

I am, Sir,
Your obedient servant,
F. G. L. Bertram,

Deputy Director of Civil Aviation."

Wilson replied a couple of days later with a letter which read in part, ". . . all this is probably true, but I wish to point out at this very moment that the Houston Expedition flyers are making daily flights over Nepalese territory."

The Air Ministry wrote to him again and this time they did not mince their words. Their second letter, dated May 15th, read:

"Dear Sir,
With reference to your letter of 10th May it is evident that you have completely misunderstood the position.

The recent Everest flight expedition obtained permission to fly over Nepalese territory only after elaborate negotiations with the Nepalese Government by the Government of India, who required special undertakings to be given.

The India Office, therefore, when we wrote concerning your proposed flight to Purnea, asked us to warn you that you cannot be permitted to fly across the frontier without the consent of the Nepalese Government, which, they added, was not likely to be forthcoming.

For this reason it is quite impossible for the Air Ministry to give you any encouragement with regard to a flight to Mount Everest involving crossing Nepalese Territory.
Yours faithfully,
F. G. L. Bertram,
Deputy Director of Civil Aviation."

Wilson was disconcerted, for he realized that without official co-operation the hazards of his flight would be substantially increased; but he had no intention of giving up his plans.

"The gloves are off," he told reporters. "I'm going on as planned. Stop me? They haven't got a chance!"

A last minute telegram forbidding his flight he tore up.

*   *   *

Sunday May 21st was cold but fine. Wilson lay awake as slowly the grey-pink flush of dawn spread over the eastern sky. Soon the sun shone brightly out of a sky that was clear and azure-blue. It was a perfect day for flying.

Laughter rang out gaily across the Stag Lane airfield, as Wilson, in the best of spirits, talked and joked with the largish crowd of people who had come to wish him Godspeed. There were reporters by the dozen, Press photographers by the score. Nigel Tangye was there, wearing a dark leather flying jacket that Wilson had given him the evening before. So was Jean Batten, the famous New Zealand pilot whose route Wilson was partially to follow. Enid and Leonard Evans were among the last he said good-bye to, and Enid tied a small square of mauve ribbon to one of the wing struts—"just for luck," she said. Finally Wilson pulled out a red and white silk pennant which he asked his friends to sign. "This is my flag of friendship," he told them. "I won't let it out of my sight." He clambered into the cockpit, "Don't worry," he shouted. "If you don't hear from me for a couple of days." The engine burst into life, the chocks were pulled away and "Ever Wrest" went lurching across the airfield.

It was not an auspicious take-off. The crowd clustered along the tarmac were horrified to see "Ever Wrest" hurtling across the airfield not up-wind but down. In the excitement of what should have been a moving and dramatic moment, Wilson had forgotten one of the basic rules of flying. He tried to take off with the wind behind him. The plane gathered speed, but it seemed an age before the tail lifted. Even then the Moth was practically on the airfield perimeter before it became airborne. But at last it rose into the air, missed a hedge by less than a couple of feet, and then climbed slowly to 2,000 feet. Then it headed south-south-east, into the morning sun. Gradually it dwindled in size until it became a mere pin-point in the bright morning sky. At last it disappeared.

The crowd on Stag Lane airfield slowly broke up. Many of them had an uneasy feeling that they would never see Wilson again.

The country was not over-excited by Wilson's departure—public enthusiasm was to come later as, contrary to all expectations, his flight towards Everest was accomplished step by step. Nevertheless articles appeared in almost all the national newspapers, and reporters, anxious to learn more about the man and his lone fantastic quest, interviewed his mother in Bradford. Wilson had told her no details of his plans, he had indeed left without even bidding her a definite good-bye. To the reporters she poured out all the fears of a loving and anxious mother.

"I have one great fear," she told them. "His left arm is practically useless. I keep asking myself, can it stand the strain? He can't carry anything heavy with it. I am terribly worried about the oxygen apparatus he will have to carry. I am afraid it might be too heavy.

"I have been very ill and I know he did not want to worry me unduly; I expect he left without saying good-bye because he thought the leave-taking might upset me."

When they asked her whether she really believed that he could climb Mount Everest alone, she only smiled and said:

"My son is a very brave man."

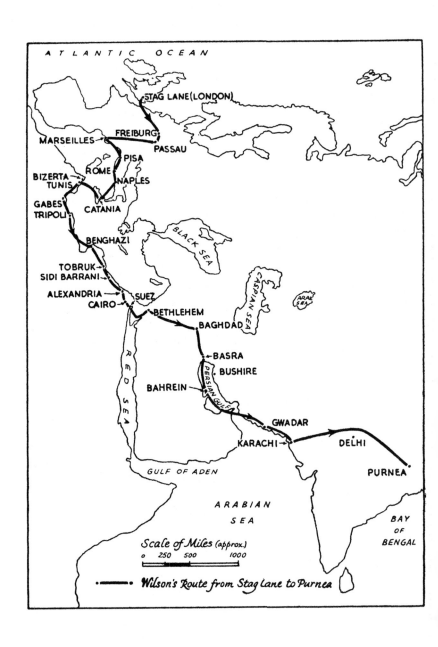

ATLANTIC OCEAN

STAG LANE (LONDON)

FREIBURG
MARSEILLES
PASSAU
PISA
ROME
BIZERTA
TUNIS
NAPLES
GABES
TRIPOLI
CATANIA
BLACK SEA
BENGHAZI
TOBRUK
SIDI BARRANI
CASPIAN SEA
ALEXANDRIA
ARAL SEA
CAIRO
SUEZ
BETHLEHEM
BAGHDAD
BASRA
BUSHIRE
RED SEA
BAHREIN
PERSIAN GULF
GWADAR
KARACHI
DELHI
PURNEA
GULF OF ADEN

ARABIAN

SEA

BAY
OF
BENGAL

Scale of Miles (approx.)
0   250   500   1000

•——— Wilson's Route from Stag Lane to Purnea

CHAPTER FIVE

A MINOR EPIC
IN THE HISTORY OF THE AIR

Wilson TODAY is remembered, if he is remembered at all, as a man who failed. It is his challenge to Everest and his death among the ice crevasses of the 23,000-foot North Col that linger most in our memory. Yet his career was in one respect outstandingly successful. His flight to Purnea was a minor epic in the history of aviation; a feat all the more remarkable because it was carried out not with the co-operation of the authorities but in the face of their every effort to stop him.

It is difficult for us today to realize that only some twenty-five years ago to fly solo to India was a considerable achievement. To see Wilson's flight in its true perspective we must be able to picture both his plane and the meagre facilities for long-distance flying that were then in existence.

His aircraft was a Gipsy Moth; a light two-seater aircraft, the passenger's cockpit being fitted with a twenty-gallon petrol tank and the pilot's cockpit being open. Its wing span was only thirty feet and its overall length less than twenty-four feet. The cruising speed was a little over eighty-five miles per hour, and the range—without the extra fuel tanks—was slightly less than four hundred miles; its endurance—again without the extra tanks—was considerably less than five hours (the makers give the practical endurance as only three-and-a-half to four hours). These figures could of course be improved on by a careful and skilful pilot, using extra tanks and taking advantage of local conditions. But, even so, few men would have cared to fly the Moth for distances of over five hundred miles or for longer than six hours.

And if Wilson's aircraft seems to our modern eyes a frail

and primitive machine, then the conditions under which he flew it must seem even more archaic. For the vast and complex organization now known loosely as "flying control" was practically non-existent in 1933. The use of radio, the benefit of accurate weather forecasts, and the thousand-and-one aids to bad weather flying that pilots now take for granted, none of these could come to Maurice Wilson's aid. Flying in those days was largely a matter of endurance and a flair for not getting lost. If he was flying to a planned route, accurate navigation and skill at map-reading were in 1933 far more important to a flyer than they are today; and in both these respects Wilson could be regarded as a good pilot. The log of "Ever Wrest" indicates that he worked out his courses carefully and accurately, and his flight was very far from being the slap-happy affair that some people seemed to consider it—indeed had he shown a quarter of the carelessness he was credited with, he would never have lived to reach the Mediterranean, let alone the north-east corner of India.

Another benefit to modern pilots that was not available to Wilson is the system of servicing and refuelling that now functions automatically on most aerodromes. In Wilson's day the number of airports at which a plane could undergo routine inspection and overhaul was strictly limited; and the fact that "Ever Wrest" received only two such inspections during five thousand miles added much to the danger of Wilson's flight; and the petrol he tipped into the long-suffering plane often came out of rusty old containers, nor was it always of a sufficiently high octane.

During most of Wilson's flight then, we must picture him muffled up in the cramped and open cockpit of "Ever Wrest", listening anxiously to a never-too-happy engine-beat, steering a rough compass course and peering doubtfully at the unfamiliar terrain that mile after mile fanned out in front of him.

*   *   *

After leaving Stag Lane Wilson flew straight to Heston

for Customs clearance; then he headed south-south-east across the Channel, his great adventure really about to begin. And within forty-eight hours reports began to circulate that he was missing.

He landed at Freiburg's Civil Airport a little after 3 p.m., and spent the evening with friends on the outskirts of the city. Early next morning he set out for Passau. He arrived at this little airstrip, close to the banks of the Danube, before noon. Now he could see, not so far ahead of him, the vast semi-circle of the Austrian Alps, their higher peaks wreathed in strato-cumulus. After refuelling at Passau, he climbed to 8,000 feet, and headed towards the mountains. Then, as far as the world could tell, he disappeared; nor for forty-eight hours was there any news of his whereabouts.

The papers were full of the most pessimistic reports: "Inquiries in Paris and Freiburg for news of Mr. Wilson have proved fruitless," stated Reuter. "A look-out is being kept." The *Daily Express* asked: "Has Maurice Wilson, the novice airman who set out to plant a Union Jack on Mount Everest, suffered the fate of Bert Hinkler who was killed in a crash during his flight to Australia?"

The truth was very simple and far less sensational.

Soon after leaving Passau, Wilson noticed that the cloud base was lowering; as he approached the foothills of the Alps it was down to seven thousand feet. He circled for half-an-hour over the Bavarian plateau trying to gain height and climb above the cloud, but "Ever Wrest" was too overloaded to climb to more than nine thousand feet. Wilson continued to cruise around hoping he would eventually use enough petrol to lighten the plane. He soon found, however, that the cloud was thickening; and, very prudently, he returned to Freiburg and there worked out an alternative route which skirted the northern fringe of the Alps via Lake Constance, Basle and Lake Geneva. This route he followed the next day, flying at 3,000 feet in a clear blue sky, while on his port beam the Austrian, Swiss and French Alps passed in slow succession; they were still wreathed in cloud.

It took the Press several days to catch up with his change of plan. The first to realize what had happened was the *Daily Mail*, who on May 24th printed the following report: "Mr. Maurice Wilson, the London Aero Club member who is flying to Mount Everest, is safe. He gave up the idea of flying over the Alps and intends taking the Lake Geneva, Marseilles route into Italy."

Then followed what were surely the pleasantest stages of Wilson's flight.

After skirting Lake Geneva he headed due south. To port lay first the high plateaux of Savoy, then the broken ranges of the Hautes and Basses Alps; to starboard gleaming in the midday sun, lay the silver snake of the Rhône; and below him there passed the historic towns of the Isere and Dordogne Valleys—Chamberg, Grenoble, Mirabeau and Aix. It was a perfect day. The wind blew softly from the north—a tail wind which gave "Ever Wrest" a ground speed of over a hundred miles per hour. He reached Marseilles well before it was dark and spent the night in a *pension* close to the air-field.

Next morning in blazing sunshine, he flew along the playground of Europe; first the French and then the Italian Riviera. One after another the well-wooded capes and the gold and silver beaches flashed beneath his wing-tips: Cannes, Antibes, Nice, Monaco and San Remo. At the latter he left the coastline and headed due east across the Ligurian Sea. This was the first time he had ventured beyond sight of land; but the crossing could not have gone more smoothly, and soon he saw land ahead, the Italian coast rising out of a slight sea-haze. He found to his delight that he had hit the shore at his exact destination, Pisa; and here he landed at the big Air Force base. He was given a rousing welcome by the Aeronautico Italiana; he was dined with great pomp and many toasts to his success, and after "Ever Wrest" had been refuelled the pilots plastered her fuselage with their signatures. From Pisa it took him less than a couple of hours to reach Rome and here he spent his fourth night.

(*Right*) The fuel permit
from Bahrein

(*Below*) "Ever Wrest" in
India

In Singla Bazaar

"Ever Wrest" was now due for her fifty-hour inspection, and this was duly carried out. While his plane was being serviced Wilson wrote to the Evanses. He told them that he and "Ever Wrest" were both in fine fettle. "So far," he wrote, "the trip is a piece of cake, I'm now able to keep the plane on course without looking constantly at the compass. Funny how it comes to you."

Next day, still in brilliant sunshine, he flew along the Campanian and Calabrian shores, touching down for lunch at Naples; then he cut across to Catania in Sicily which he reached a little after 3 p.m. He wanted to make the hundred-mile crossing of the Mediterranean that afternoon; he re-fuelled quickly and was soon airborne, and skirting the 10,000-foot cone of Etna. But when he came to the Marsala Strait, he found a thin white mist rising in little spirals from the sea; visibility was down to less than ten miles, and he returned to Catania for the night.

He was airborne at 6 a.m. the next day, and there soon came the first—but by no means the last—test of his ability as a pilot.

The mist had cleared a little as he approached the Strait, but it still lay here and there in thickish patches at sea-level. And over the whole of the Mediterranean there stretched a low white canopy of fleecy cloud, its base at five hundred feet. Wilson tried to climb above the cloud—a task that would have been easy enough today—but he had no oxygen, and at 9,000 feet he gave up and descended to sea level. He checked his compass and set course at three hundred feet for the invisible African shore. It was a nerve-racking trip. Every now and then "Ever Wrest" would come to a thick patch of mist too big to be skirted; the horizon would disappear and Wilson would be left flying blind, only a little above the sea-level, his eyes unable to penetrate the swirling waves of mist that rolled around him. As he neared the African coast the mist began to thicken. It occurred to Wilson, after an hour's flying, that the shore must now be very close; and he expected at any moment to see the low cliffs of Cape Bon darkening the mist. Partly by luck and partly by good judgment he hit the coast line at an angle and where it was low, and ten minutes after seeing the waves well up around the Maoin Peninsula he touched down on the sunbaked landing strip at Tunis.

It was here that his troubles really began.

He found the facilities for refuelling were not to his liking at Tunis. Curiously enough, although the airstrip was quite a large one, he found difficulty in finding anyone who spoke English and to whom he could explain his needs. He therefore took off at once and headed north-west for Bizerta, only a few miles distant, where a larger airstrip had recently been built. He touched down safely, if not very expertly, and taxied over to the dispersal point. As he clambered out of "Ever Wrest", a police car came racing across the 'drome and pulled up beside him in a cloud of dust. Three armed policemen tumbled out, told Wilson he was under arrest and pushed him into the back of their car. They drove in silence to the police station. Here Wilson waited for half an hour; then the same three policemen came in, told him to get into the car again and drove him back to "Ever Wrest".

"We are sorry," said one of them, "but you are not permitted to stay here."

"Suits me," said Wilson, "I never intended to stay."

"It would have saved us much unneccessary trouble," said the man coldly, "if you had told us that before."

It seemed pointless to argue.

"Can I refuel my plane?" asked Wilson mildly.

"No!" said the policeman, "you may not."

Wilson realized that any argument would probably land him in a Bizerta cell, so he clambered into his plane, returned to Tunis, refuelled "Ever Wrest" himself from a stock of rather rusty-looking drums and set course, with considerable misgivings along the Tunisian shore.

The north coast of Africa is one of the bleakest, most barren areas of the world; mile after mile of monotonous desert, with little outcrops of rock, occasional patches of scrub, and vast areas of drab, colourless sand. For long distances it is quite waterless and quite uninhabited. A forced landing here would have meant almost certain death, and Wilson listened with more than usual anxiety to the steady engine-beat of his Moth. It sounded, at first, reassuringly smooth. But after he had left Gabes some dozen miles astern and was nearing the Libyan border, it began to roughen and cough; soon a violent knocking began to jar through the whole plane. Wilson quickly throttled back, turned through 180°, and slowly losing height, headed back for Gabes. He landed safely, and as he was taxiing across the airstrip, his engine gave a final splutter and cut.

"Your fuel had water in it!" a mechanic later told him. "You're lucky to be alive."

The rest of his flight over Africa was monotonous, but mercifully uneventful.

Once his fuel had been drained off and renewed, he flew on, hour after hour, parallel to the shore. The weather was still fine, but flying conditions were far from pleasant; for the sun blazed hotly out of a brazen sky, its glare seared his eyes and blistered his face, and the air along the coastline was rough and turbulent; "Ever Wrest" kept lurching into air-pockets and little areas of turbulence. But one by one the desert air-strips were left behind him: Gabes, Tripoli, Benghazi, Tobruk and Sidi Barrani, and at last the green thread of the Nile Valley pencilled across his perspex windscreen. He landed at Cairo exactly a week after leaving Stag Lane. He was right on schedule.

"So far, so good," he wrote to Leonard Evans. But his real test was still to come.

Wilson had been told, when he first worked out his route, that he would need a permit to fly over Persian territory. He had applied for this permit, and five weeks before his departure from Stag Lane he was officially notified that it had come through. The permit would, he was told, be waiting for him in Cairo. But when, from Cairo airport, he telephoned the British Legation to ask where he should pick the document up, he received an unpleasant surprise.

The phone was first answered by a clerk who seemed to know all about his inquiry.

"Oh yes, Mr. Wilson," came the reassuring words, "I think there's something here for you."

Then suddenly the line went dead, and when Wilson was re-connected it was to an older man that he spoke.

"I'm sorry, old man," he was told, "I'm afraid there's no permit for you here. If there's any way I can help," the voice added sympathetically, "just let me know."

This was a set-back Wilson had never bargained for. He spent twenty-four hours in Cairo, being passed on from one Government department to the next. He tried to be reasonable, he tried to bluster, but the result was always the same evasive answer, and the suggestion that some other official might be in a better position to help him. Wilson remembered his brush with the Air Ministry, and the warnings he had so lightly ignored when he was still in England; and it came to him that the disappearance of his permit might well be a deliberate attempt to halt his progress. Certain government departments might, he knew, be more than a little embarrassed were he to arrive suddenly in India; they might imagine that by withholding his Persian permit they could stop him.

But when Wilson had told reporters, "Stop me? They haven't got a chance!" his boast had been no idle one. He began to plan an alternative route, though a glance at the map will show that this was no easy task; for the six hundred thousand square miles of Persian territory lay sprawled directly across his route; to skirt them to the north he would have to fly over the Caspian Sea and the towering Elburz Mountains, while to the south lay one of the hottest and most desolate areas of the world—the Persian Gulf and the East Arabian desert. He decided he would push on to Baghdad, close to the Persian border, and there try again to find the mislaid permit, though he felt certain in his own mind that it was languishing—and not by accident—in some official's pigeon-hole.

At the Cairo airport "Ever Wrest" was given a thorough inspection and servicing—her last for some months: then Wilson flew the thousand-odd miles to Baghdad in a single day, with brief calls at Suez, Gaza, Bethlehem and Gadda *en route*. The last part of his journey, across the Trans-Jordan plateau, was particularly difficult; mile after mile the desert upland stretched out before him, with scarcely a single distinguishing feature; but Wilson's compass flying was, by this time, extremely accurate and he arrived safely at Baghdad half an hour before sunset.

Here he again made inquiries about his permit, and when it became obvious that this would not be forthcoming, tried to obtain a fresh one. But it soon became clear that permission to fly over Persia would never be given. If he landed there, even to refuel, without a permit he would be arrested; so there was only one thing to do; change his route and fly round the formidable barrier.

His first necessity was maps, and he soon found that these were about the only thing in Baghdad it was almost impossible to buy! He eventually ran to earth a tattered school atlas and a survey sheet for the north-western section of the Persian Gulf. He worked out that Baghdad to Basra was three hundred miles, and Basra to the Island of Bahrein (a British Protectorate in the Persian Gulf) four hundred miles. Each of these "legs" was of quite a reasonable length, and his spirits rose. Then, almost by chance, he heard that the airstrip at Basra was closed.

He was faced now by a flight of seven hundred miles, a distance very close to his plane's maximum range, and the second part of it over some of the most desolate country in the world. And for the last two hundred miles he had no map. A less courageous man would probably have turned back; but Wilson was now to show that streak of obstinate courage—some would call it rash stupidity—that was later to reach its full flowering on the upper slopes of Everest.

He took off from Baghdad and headed south-south-east. If he lost his way, even for twenty minutes, he would be faced with the prospect of an unpleasant, blistering death on the Persian shore.

Wilson worked out that the flight would take a little over nine hours; he therefore made an early start and was airborne at 7.30 a.m., less than an hour after sunrise. His track at first was easy to keep to, for it criss-crossed over the loops of the Tigris flood plain. Beneath him stretched a maze of canals and irrigated paddy fields, and away to starboard the sun glinted dully on the slow-moving River Euphrates. But after about a hundred miles the Tigris wound away to the left and the Euphrates to the right, and Wilson felt very much alone. Soon he passed over the Ruins of Narfer, on the fringe of Lake Hor-al-Afaq, and he realized he had drifted a little off-course. He checked his compass and altered course 5° to port; and soon the great swamp of the Basra Delta fanned out before him; an hour later he could see, far ahead, the sheen of sunlight on the Persian Gulf. He passed over Basra at eleven-twenty and knew that he was not yet half-way to the Island of Bahrein.

Over the shore of the Gulf the heat struck him like the banked-up flames of a blast furnace. His face, already tanned a deep bronze, now seamed into tiny painful cracks; and soon the golden shore line began to dance with fantastic mirages. Hour after hour he flew on, twelve miles off-shore and parallel to the Arabian desert. The sun beat down, searing into his eyes and sending dull shafts of pain across the back of his neck. The water was a dull metallic blue; utterly without movement, utterly without trace of life; it lay as if ironed flat by the molten heat waves of the sun.

It was like a journey without end; and as the seventh hour passed slowly into the eighth, Wilson felt himself becoming light-headed with fatigue. Then, after eight-and-a-half hours' flying, he saw a faint shadow, very far ahead, darken the waters of the Gulf; and twenty minutes later he landed on Bahrein's newly-built and sun-drenched airstrip.

He staggered to bed at once with a splitting headache, but told the mechanics to refuel his plane that evening.

"I'm taking off again," he said, "at dawn."

Wilson had yet to learn that the arm of Authority is long. The next morning his fuel tanks were still empty and he was told that he had been refused petrol on the instructions of the British Consul.

With some justification Wilson felt that the authorities had over-reached themselves. His plane was airworthy and his pilot's certificate in order. He had, in the first instance, asked for all the necessary permits for his flight and had been told officially that these would be available. When one permit had failed to materialize as promised, he had, at considerable personal risk, flown by an alternative route. He had committed no crime and had broken no law. What justification, he asked, had the airport authorities for refusing him petrol? Did they expect him and his plane to stay stranded on Bahrein for ever?

Getting a good deal of sympathy but no petrol at the airport, Wilson called on the British Consulate. Here an official told him that he was forbidden to continue his flight since he had no permit to fly over Persian territory.

"But I haven't flown over Persian territory," Wilson pointed out. "Nor do I intend to!"

The official smiled suavely. "What type of plane are you flying, Mr. Wilson?" he asked.

"A Gipsy Moth."

"And what is the maximum range of this particular plane?"

"About seven hundred and fifty miles."

"Exactly, Mr. Wilson! Apart from Baghdad, where you've just come from, there is no airstrip within seven hundred and fifty miles of Bahrein that is not in Persian territory. We know, you see, where you must be heading."

Wilson threw up his hands in despair. "Can I take a look at your map?" he finally asked.

"With pleasure."

Wilson studied the large-scale map of the Persian Gulf that hung on the office wall; he memorized its scale and its details, while the official, smiling smugly, leant over his shoulder. As he turned away Wilson jotted down half-a-dozen figures on the cuff of his khaki shirt. An idea began to form in his mind.

Now Wilson was not by nature a deceitful man. But neither was he a man who lay down meekly under what he thought to be injustice. Rightly or wrongly he thought that the authorities were treating him unfairly—"They tried," he wrote later to Enid Evans, "to do the dirty on me"—and he considered he had every justification for trying to outwit them. With a show of resignation he said he would accept the official's ruling. He asked him his advice and the two men, that afternoon, went out together for tea.

"What do you think I should do?" Wilson asked.

"If I were you," the reply came quickly, "I'd fly to Bushire—that's the nearest Persian drome. You could land and ask them for a permit there."

Wilson hid his anger. He knew very well that once he landed in Persia, with the permit not actually in his possession, "Ever Wrest" would be impounded and he himself imprisoned.

"I suppose you're right," he said with a smile. "Will you write me out a fuel chit?"

"Yes, of course, old man. Call in tomorrow for it."

"And perhaps you'd loan me a couple of maps?"

"Can't let you take 'em away. Why not make copies?"

"That would do fine."

Next morning Wilson called early at the Consulate and an official wrote out the following chit:

MR. WILSON   G-ABJC.   MOTH

You are permitted to refuel and leave Bahrein on the understanding that you proceed direct to Bushire.

You should keep outside the three-mile limit of the Hasa Coast.   P. A. Bahrein.

And while this was being written, Wilson made hurried notes from the map that hung on the Consulate wall. It was a large map and extended westward into Iran and eastward into Baluchistan. The official failed to notice that Wilson took most of his details from the extreme south-eastern corner.

Once he had the fuel chit Wilson hurried back to the 'drome, and an hour later, at a little after 10 a.m., he was ready to leave. The official was there to see him off.

"Bye-bye, old man," he called out as Wilson taxied past him.

Wilson wished he could have seen the official's face, as, once he was airborne, he turned the nose of his plane, not northward for Bushire but due east for Baluchistan and Everest.

And so began the last and most amazing stage of his flight to the borders of India.

While in the Consulate Wilson had noticed on the wall-map that a newly-built airstrip was marked at Gwadar, a small Baluchistan town a few miles beyond the Persian frontier. He had jotted down on his cuff the scale of the map, and later he worked out that Gwadar was a little less than eight hundred miles from Bahrein—only just beyond the Moth's effective range.

He had no map; the track he would have to fly along lay almost entirely over the sea, and out of sight of land; and if —as seemed very probable—he ran out of petrol and crashed there would be little chance of his survival.

Wilson decided to take the risk.

He took his petrol permit to the airstrip, and while the plane was being refuelled he talked one of the native mechanics into selling him a small extra drum which he hid in "Ever Wrest's" front storage locker. Then he took off.

The distance he had to cover was in fact seven hundred and seventy miles, the exact range of "Ever Wrest" taking her extra fuel drum into account. There was no room for the slightest margin of error.

For nine-and-a-half hours Wilson flew almost due east,

on a course of 095°. After three-quarters of an hour he passed over the tip of the Quatar Peninsula and was able to check his course. He reckoned he was drifting a little to starboard and altered course accordingly. Then for nearly five hours, out of sight of land, he flew over the burnished waters of the Persian Gulf. He saw nothing, except once a handful of native dhows, apparently becalmed in the glass-like sea. Hour after hour he flew on, into the stifling heat.

Suddenly, for no apparent reason, the engine began to cough, then it cut completely. Wilson was flying at two thousand feet. His mind flashed back to his engine failure in England; the fields of Yorkshire had been beneath him then, but now it was towards the vast emptiness of the sea that his plane began to fall. He checked his fuel-cock and engine switches; then began to carry out the drill for re-starting an engine in height. Already he was down to fifteen hundred feet. He put the nose still further down. The wind sighed through his struts, and as for the first time he pulled "Ever Wrest" out of her dive the engine gave a single staccato cough, then again there was silence. Wilson muttered a prayer. It seemed that only a miracle could save him. He was now down to less than one thousand feet. For what he knew would be his last attempt, he pushed the nose down; at one hundred and fifty feet he pulled the plane out of the dive; the engine coughed, faltered, then suddenly burst into life. "Ever Wrest" skimmed low over the water, then rose in a steady climb toward the safety of the sky.

"I prayed," Wilson afterwards wrote, "and my prayer was answered."

He might equally well have said, "I remembered my starting drill, and it worked."

After a little over five hours he saw a narrow neck of low-lying land jutting out across his path. Wilson sighed with relief. It was the Ras-el-Jebe Peninsula, which divides the Gulf of Persia from the Gulf of Oman. Here he was able to check both his track and the progress he was making. He found he was exactly on course, but ten minutes behind schedule. Doggedly he pushed on. Soon, once again, he was out of sight of land.

He was flying over the Indian Ocean now, his course very gradually converging with the South-east Persian shore; soon he saw the shadow of its outline, fifty miles distant on his port bow.

After seven hours in the air Wilson began to suffer agonies from cramp. He was a big man, and "Ever Wrest's" cockpit was small. He could not stretch out his legs to ease the pain without putting pressure on the rudder and swinging "Ever Wrest" off course. Soon the sweat of his agony was added to the heat sweat which had already soaked his khaki shirt and shorts. After a little the pain wore off, but Wilson was left exhausted.

After eight hours he would have welcomed back the cramp to overcome his utter weariness. He had to fight now against a terrible drowsiness that gradually seeped into him. Several times his eyes closed, and he nodded off at the controls, and "Ever Wrest" veered off course. Once he pulled her out of a screaming dive less than two hundred feet above the sea.

After nine hours he could see ahead of him the grey haze of impending night. Darkness falls quickly in the tropics, and Wilson knew that yet another hazard would soon be threatening him. He checked his petrol and realized there was very little left.

Then, after nine hours and ten minutes in the air, he saw fanning out ahead the coast of India. He flew low over the mangrove and paddy fields, and twenty minutes later saw the white buildings of Gwadar airstrip, outlined by long shadows, standing like a mirage in the path of the setting sun.

As he came in to land his engine began to cough. There was not enough petrol in his tank to cover an upended sixpence, and ten minutes later it was quite dark.

*   *   *

It had taken Wilson a little under a fortnight to cover the

five thousand miles to India; a great achievement for a man with so little flying experience.

Yet his adventures had, in fact, only just begun; and he was to overcome many and even more formidable obstacles before he finally set foot on Everest.

That first night in India he ate a huge meal, then went to sleep in the open; and the next day he began his flight to Purnea. His eyes were red and sore after his ordeal of the day before, and for the next week he took things very quietly, flying in easy stages from one airport to the next—Karachi, Hyderabad, Jodhpur, Allahabad, and finally Lalbalu, a military aerodrome only nine miles from Purnea. Twice more he was refused petrol, apparently on Government orders. Once he flew to a neighbouring 'drome and refuelled there, and the other time he persuaded an Irish hotel keeper to show him where the airport's fuel was stored. He re-fuelled "Ever Wrest" himself, during the night, leaving the correct money beneath a stone at the entrance to the fuel store.

It was getting on for the middle of June when Wilson landed at Lalbalu. During the last few days of his flight across India the Press had again caught up with him, and wherever he landed Wilson was interviewed and photographed. Now that, in the face of all official forecasts, he had reached India alive, his fantastic quest began to be taken far more seriously.

The *Daily Express* printed a long article, which their special correspondent had wired them after an interview at Karachi. "Maurice Wilson," it read, "the young Bradford airman and rock climber who has undertaken the amazing adventure of a combined aerial and foot climb of Everest, gave some re-markable details of his plan when he landed here after flying from England. 'Enough rice and dates to last fifty days,' he said, 'will be in my rucksack when I begin to climb Everest after landing on the mountain some 14,000 feet up. One fit, trained man can succeed where a large group have failed. For ten months I have trained, testing foods and special types of fasts until I have found that the best procedure is to take one meal a day; this will enable me to breathe deep down in my stomach, taking in a vastly increased supply of oxygen.' His ten months of training and experimenting," the correspondent added, "have given him the utmost confidence. He considers his optimism fully justified, as he has read every known book and studied every known map of Everest in that period. He said he will carry a sealed oxygen apparatus, but will not use it unless he is absolutely forced to. 'There is no stunt about it,' Mr. Wilson reiterated. 'Mine is a carefully planned expedition.' "

Other papers carried equally long articles. To *The Statesman* Wilson gave details of the equipment he would use on the mountain. "Asked about equipment, Mr. Wilson produced various warm garments made specially to order for him; all were of the lightest woollen material. His whole kit weighs only forty pounds, including the tent, sleeping bag, outer suit of warm light material lined with silk and made to resist wind, sun and water, and a series of woollen cardigans. The unique feature of his climbing outfit is his boots, made with insulated cork, running from toe to heel."

Almost all these Press articles spoke highly of Wilson's determination, and his obviously careful planning. After his amazing flight to India it seemed almost as if he might succeed. But within a few days of his arrival at Lalbalu, *The Statesman* printed a small paragraph which was to hold the key to the next nine months. "In discussing his venture Mr. Wilson admitted that one point alone he had never properly considered—the question of receiving permission to fly over or into Nepal. It did not strike him at first that this would be an immense barrier, but . . . so far he has failed to obtain permission."

First, Wilson had been refused a permit to fly over Persia; now, it seemed, he would be refused a permit to fly into Nepal. It had taken him only a few days to surmount the first obstacle, but it was to be a matter of nearly nine months before he overcame the second.

CHAPTER SIX

FRUSTRATION

Soon after Wilson had touched down at Lalbalu he received a visit from the local Chief of Police and the two men formed an instant liking for one another; but the latter had received certain very definite instructions and he eventually came to the point and served Wilson with an official notice, ordering the Yorkshireman to bring "Ever Wrest" into Purnea and then restraining him from further flying. When Wilson asked the reason for this, he was told, unofficially, that the authorities intended to make quite certain he never flew into Nepal without the necessary permit.

Wilson resigned himself to the delay—the season for climbing Everest was already drawing to its close, and he must have known that his attempt would in any case have to be postponed.

He was told to fly his plane into a compound owned by the Maharaja of Durbhanga. But he quickly realized that "Ever Wrest", when fully loaded with all his equipment, was too heavy to land safely on the Maharaja's miniature landing field. He therefore stripped the plane down, stored all his personal effects, and the next day flew "Ever Wrest" safely in. He was met by a police guard, and was told that the plane would be kept under constant surveillance. He was told too, much to his indignation, that he would be expected to pay for the guard—and indeed the latter cost him three rupees a day during his stay in Lalbalu.

During the next few weeks Wilson made constant appeals both to the British and Nepalese authorities, for permission to fly over Nepal to Everest. At last he was told he could go to Raxall, on the border of Nepal, where his case would be considered.

The monsoon had broken now; and Wilson was hampered in his cross-country journey by high wind and slanting rain. It took him twenty-four hours to cover the two hundred miles to Raxall; and he might just as well have stayed in Lalbalu, for though the authorities must surely have realized that the breaking of the monsoon precluded any attempt on Everest, no permit was forthcoming. Wilson met several officials in Raxall and went three miles over the border to Birganj where he despatched a wire to Khatmandu to the Maharaja of Nepal. He waited three days for a reply and when it came it was a politely-phrased refusal. He telephoned Khatmandu and was met with another and not-so-polite refusal. "No!" an official told him. "You can't fly over Nepal, and if you telephone ten times a day for the next ten years the answer will still be 'No'!"

Wilson was bitterly disappointed. He studied the approaches to Everest with the greatest care, and came reluctantly to the conclusion that without crossing Nepalese territory there was no way of approaching the mountain by air.

Yet never for a moment did he think of turning back. He was, to his way of thinking, not embarking on an adventure but answering a Divine call. A theory had to be proved, and to prove it he had to climb Mount Everest alone. The more obstacles that were put in his way, the more determined he became. His lone assault began to turn slowly into a magnificent obsession. And, if further spur were needed to strengthen his resolve it now came; for news seeped out that the Ruttledge expedition had been forced to turn back, and was now on its way to Darjeeling. Everest was still inviolate; the ultimate challenge.

Wilson wondered at first whether he could trick the authorities into releasing his plane. He toyed with the idea of telling them he had decided to travel to Everest by foot, via Sikkim and Tibet, and asking if he might use his plane for preliminary reconnaissance work; then, once airborne, he would head straight into Nepal. But the weather now was far too uncertain for Himalayan flying, and this idea he reluctantly put aside. Various other schemes he also rejected, one after another, as impracticable.

In the meanwhile he settled down to life in Purnea. He found it "a delightful place . . . full of retired people, and I don't blame them for living in such a wonderful spot—it must be the only bit of green in India, I think . . . apart from the Government officials, the kindness and hospitality of everyone has been quite overwhelming." But as his enforced stay lengthened from weeks to months, Wilson began to find himself in some financial embarrassment. He spent very little on food, living almost entirely on rice, oats and bananas; but the cost of his board and lodging and the guard he still had to pay for watching "Ever Wrest" gradually mounted up, and he wrote late in June that he had only "twenty quid left in the whole wide world". It gradually came to him that he had in fact only one realizable asset— his plane—and that was lashed down in the open, exposed to the monsoon rains, and was deteriorating fast.

It was about this time that he received an invitation to visit a certain Major Kent, whose plantation was at Purtabpore some two hundred and fifty miles from Lalbalu. He decided to fly there; but "Ever Wrest" had been sadly neglected in the last few weeks and refused to start.

Wilson now gave proof of his resource and ingenuity. He rummaged among his papers and found an engine handling booklet; with this propped up on the windscreen he set to work on the engine, and carried out routine inspection and overhaul. It took him over five hours, but at the end he was rewarded when the engine spluttered into life and was soon, according to Wilson, "giving better revs than it had since delivery from the makers".

"Ever Wrest" was wheeled on to the airstrip. But the take-off run was short and the field wet and sodden, and Wilson realized that the plane was not likely to leave the ground in time. Not to be outdone he found another booklet, this time on aircraft rigging, and set to work with a will. He carried out a number of major modifications and a couple of days later took off safely.

Wilson spent several days with Kent, but the latter's air-

Karma Paul

(*Above*) The Rongbuk Monastery

(*Left*) The Head Lama of Rongbuk

strip had no hangar, and Wilson was now becoming seriously worried about the effect of continuously leaving "Ever Wrest" exposed to the weather. Very regretfully he made up his mind that since there now seemed no possibility of his flying to the foot of Everest, he must resign himself to selling her, and covering the rest of his journey by foot. It was a hard decision to make, for the Moth had never failed him, and Wilson had developed a sentimental affection for the plane which had carried him safely a third of the way round the world. He received many offers for "Ever Wrest" which had now of course become famous, and eventually he sold her for five hundred pounds to a man he particularly liked— a planter named Cassells. And with this sale the first phase of his lone assault on Everest drew to its successful close.

*   *   *

At the end of July, having delivered "Ever Wrest" to Cassells at the U.P. Flying Club in Lucknow, Wilson set out for Darjeeling—the starting-off point of all Everest expeditions. He had as yet no definite plans; but at the back of his mind was the feeling that having been forbidden the direct route via Nepal, he could only hope to approach Everest from the flank, via Sikkim and Tibet.

It was pleasant well-wooded country he travelled through, and as the miniature railway carried him high into the Himalayan foothills his spirits rose. Darjeeling itself delighted him.

He found the town lying among the foothills of an arm of the Himalaya, which reach out southward into India. It was a little more than seven thousand feet above sea level, and to the north and west rose a chain of towering peaks, dominated by the massive block of Kangchenjunga. Often, as Wilson soon found, the town was shrouded in mist or rain, but it was a cool mist, blown straight from the Himalayan snows, and very different to the sultry humidity of the Indian plains.

Darjeeling has a closer association with Everest than any

other town; almost all Everest expeditions recruit porters
here for at least the initial stages of their three hundred mile
trek to the base of the mountain, and every expedition
between the two world wars made a start from this surprisingly cosmopolitan and modern town.

Wilson soon settled into a small hotel in Darjeeling and
at once began to plan his one-man expedition for the coming
spring. It was obvious from the start that the authorities
would give him neither help nor advice. He applied for a
permit to enter Sikkim and Tibet on foot and was bluntly
refused. He therefore began to make preparations in secret
and his first step was to find a guide.

Here it seemed that fate played right into Wilson's hands;
for he was introduced one evening to Karma Paul.

Karma Paul was a Tibetan, born in 1899 in Lhasa. He
was a well-educated man who could speak seven languages,
and he had served in the 1922, 1924 and 1933 Expeditions,
in the last as an official interpreter. He told Wilson a great
deal about the approaches to Everest, and eventually suggested that he should accompany the Yorkshireman as far
as the site of the previous expeditions' Base Camp.

This on the face of it seemed an attractive proposition,
and at first Wilson readily agreed. Karma Paul painted an
encouraging picture of Tibet, as a land where Wilson would
find plenty of food along his route and a shelter of sorts in
which to pass most nights; and the Yorkshireman could now
see his way clear to arriving at the foot of Everest by next
spring; once there he would wait for the onset of favourable
weather, and then, he believed, his philosophy of self-
discipline would carry him to the summit.

But it gradually became apparent that Wilson and
Karma Paul did not, on a great number of points, see eye to
eye; and what was even more important, they did not particularly like one another. Wilson was a difficult man to get
on with, and after several months of uneasy partnership they
agreed to part. Wilson felt that Karma Paul was unreliable—
he had promised to call personally on the Dalai Lama at

Lhasa and ask for Wilson's permit to travel through Tibet, and this promise was never fulfilled. Karma Paul felt that Wilson's ideas were too unorthodox for safety. The judgment of both men was probably sound.

As winter approached, Wilson's plans began to crystallize. He had by this time quite lost hope of obtaining official permits to travel through Sikkim or Tibet, and he began to map out a route which he could follow, disguised as a Tibetan priest. He knew that priests were able to travel without permits, and he hoped that he would in a few months' time have learnt enough of the Tibetan language to pass a casual inspection. To make doubly sure that he was not caught by the police and brought ignominiously back, he decided to travel entirely by night.

Towards the end of October Wilson applied for permission to join a small party, who were planning a ten days' tour of the Sikkim foothills and much to his surprise, permission was granted. Wilson was overjoyed.

It turned out, however, that the "permission" was something of a trap. Three times while he was away the Darjeeling police paid surprise visits to his lodgings; they wanted to assure themselves that his equipment was still there. And twice a Sikkim policeman caught up with the touring party to make certain that Wilson was still with them Had there been the slightest hint of his making a surprise dash to Everest, the police would certainly have cast their net to bring him quickly back.

But Wilson had no immediate deep-laid schemes. He travelled through the Sikkim foothills admiring the grandeur of the scenery, his mind untroubled by any thoughts of the future: the present was too enjoyable.

He found the scenery very like that of the Southern Alps on the west coast of New Zealand, only on a far grander scale. Great ice-fluted peaks rose all around them to a height of 20,000 feet, and between these lay semi-tropical valleys whose floor was only some two to three thousand feet above sea-level.

The party travelled at first through woods of oak, fir and beech; but gradually these gave way to a more open landscape, with dark green terraces of tea interspersed with belts of tall bamboo. Then the going grew rougher, as their track wound through the great primeval forests at the head of a steep-sided valley. Wilson—who was something of an amateur botanist—identified many trees which might, were it not for their incredible size, have been lifted straight from an English garden: oak and maple, birch and rhododendron: laurel and fir. But there were other trees too, intertwined in erotic profusion, which Wilson had never seen before; pepper and menispermum; vines and begonias, wild cinnamon and orchids. And it was in the silence and pale green light of the forest that they met their first leeches.

These Sikkim leeches are normally about the size of a match, but when gorged they swell quickly up to the dimensions of a large slug. They are quite blind, but have a keen sense of smell and quickly batten on any form of life. Soon the track was swarming with them, and Wilson found they seemed to have no difficulty in boring through his clothing and fixing on his skin. They were the only serpents in Paradise.

It was at the end of the third day that Wilson caught his first glimpse of Everest—a distant fang of white, half veiled in passing cloud. He would have preferred at this first sight of his objective to be alone, and the reference in his diary to what should have been a moving scene is almost casual. "Had a most perfect day yesterday," he wrote, "the views were marvellous and quite the best of anything I've ever seen. Had my first glimpse of Everest, but alas there was too much of a crowd about to register a true impression."

The "true impression" was to come a couple of nights later.

It had been raining almost all day, but towards evening it cleared, and Wilson decided to spend the night in the open, in his sleeping bag, while his companions slept close at hand in a small bungalow. He woke a little before dawn,

to the song of the coppersmith bird beating out its monotonous metallic note from the branch of a nearby fir.

As he raised himself on his elbow, he saw through a gap
in the mist, a great segment of white gleaming in the grey
light of morning. At first he thought it was a cloud, then he
realized it was too still, too unchanging in its outline. It was
Everest. Even as he watched, the sudden glow of dawn
swept over the upper reaches of the sky; the nearer mists
dissolved and a great semi-circle of peaks was suddenly unveiled, their summits warmed red by the titanic conflagra-
tion of dawn. And the summit of Everest rose majestically
behind them all, and when the clouds again rolled back it
was the last to disappear. The Goddess Mother of the
World was waiting.

By the end of the trip Wilson had covered over one hundred and eighty miles, and he realized with some dismay
that he was far from being one hundred per cent fit. "One
part of the trek," he wrote, "we did a straight drop down a
gulley—fourteen miles. I thought my damned knees were
never going to bend again!"

Back in Darjeeling he put himself on a strict diet: one
meal a day, consisting only of porridge, boiled barley and
green vegetables. He also started on the long walks that had
been a feature of his training in England. Then towards the
end of the year he embarked on a three weeks' fast; he would,
he said, rebuild his body anew, so that he would be worthy
both physically and mentally of his supreme test.

He broke the fast on Christmas Day, and early in January
began making definite plans for a dash to Everest some time
in March. He wrote in his diary that once he reached the
mountain he would lay-up at the Rongbuk Monastery until
the weather was good enough for his assault to begin—
"some time late in April I expect."

On January 15th there came in Wilson's routine existence
a terrible diversion. The whole of North-east India was
shaken by the most appalling earthquake. Many of the
buildings in Darjeeling partially collapsed; but the damage

here was light compared with the catastrophic disaster that
shook Nepal and Bihar. More than a hundred and twenty
thousand square miles were devastated; rivers were blocked
and vast areas became quickly flooded. The death role
mounted in a few days to over ten thousand.

In Darjeeling the work of restoration was quickly put in
hand. There was soon a shortage of labour and even the
native children were pressed into service, carrying huge
loads of earth, rubble or cement in panniers slung across
their backs. And in the heart of the most devastated areas
there could always be seen the gaunt figure of Wilson, still
weakened by his fast, but hard at work. Many Europeans
disapproved of his helping the natives in their manual
labour, but Wilson, apart from any humanitarian motive,
wanted to build up his body, and develop the muscles that
were, he thought, to carry him to the roof of the world.

Towards the end of January Wilson, having definitely
parted company with Karma Paul, began to look round for
another guide. And this time he was lucky.

He managed to trace three Sherpa porters—Tewang,
Tsering and Rinzing—who had taken part in the Ruttledge
expedition of the year before; he still planned to make the
actual ascent of Everest alone, but he appreciated that
porters would be invaluable in guiding him to the base of the
mountain and carrying his provisions and equipment at
least as far as the Rongbuk Monastery. The three Sherpas
wanted if possible to stay together, and Wilson accordingly
engaged them all. Nor could he have made a wiser choice,
for they proved trustworthy and hard-working. And, what
is more, a bond of mutual regard and even affection came to
make their relationship a peculiarly happy one.

Acknowledgment has often been made of the noble part
played by the Sherpas in attempts on Everest and other
Himalayan peaks. It is perhaps enough to quote Frank
Smythe's remark that, "No Himalayan expedition would be
possible without them." And the three men who now
joined forces with Wilson, and who were later to play so

large a part in his assault, typified all the better qualities of a race noted for their hardiness and courage. Ruttledge said of his porters, including Tewang, Tsering and Rinzing, "I make no apology for putting on record the names of as gallant a company as ever served an expedition." He also referred to Tewang personally. "Not once did they (the porters) fail to bring hot tea and soup at the right moment. There would come a yell outside, the tent opening would be hurriedly unlaced, and the youthful Tewang dragged bodily in accompanied by a ton of snow . . . efficient, completely reliable and never idle, he performed every office from porter, messman to nurse, in a manner beyond praise."

Wilson was indeed lucky to win the services of three such loyal and experienced men.

He now began to plan his exact route and mode of travel. He acquired, sometimes by rather questionable methods, a vast collection of maps covering the approaches to Everest. Over these he and Tewang pored, hour after hour; until Wilson felt certain that they knew the little-used track they had decided to follow so well that they could find it even in the dark. It was a route that lay mostly over the high wind-swept Tibetan plateau, a route that would tax his endurance to the uttermost—"might have to swim a couple of big rivers dodging the police," he wrote. "It would be just too humorous to be returned to Darjeeling under police escort."

He bought a small but sturdy Sikkim pony, which he intended to ride along the easier stretches. When the authorities asked him what the pony was for, he said he was riding it at a tiger-shoot to which a friend had invited him. And, as a further red herring, he paid the rent for his rooms six months in advance.

His disguise was obviously a matter of great importance, and here again he enlisted the help of the Sherpas. They entered whole-heartedly into the spirit of the scheme, and managed to collect an imposing array of garments. A few weeks before they planned to leave Wilson staged a dress rehearsal. He paraded laughingly in his new clothes, which consisted, from top to bottom, of a fur-lined Bhutia cap, with huge ear-flaps, a magnificent waistcoat, brocaded in gold (but with enormous buttons of brass!); trousers of cheap dark-blue cotton, and round his middle a twelve-foot sash of pure, vivid-red silk. Over all he wore a heavy woollen mantle of navy-blue, which hung down to his feet. He insisted on retaining his hobnail cork-insulated boots, but to hide his blue-grey eyes, wore dark glasses. The mantle was caught up in his sash so forming voluminous pockets, which Wilson improved with his needle and cotton.

His flying and mountaineering kit he packed carefully into two thirty-pound packs, which the Sherpas were to carry until he could travel without disguise.

He fixed a definite date for slipping unseen out of Darjeeling—March 21st. And this time he kept to it.

And so, almost a year after leaving England, his lone attempt on Everest now took definite shape.

*   *   *

Wilson was to lose his life for an ideal. It could be argued that the ideal was not worth the sacrifice; that is a matter of opinion. What cannot be denied is that Wilson knew what he was doing. Nor is there any doubt that had he succeeded he would have won for his particular belief a world-wide following. Unless there is something inherently evil in the ideals of others, it behoves us not to trample on them with hobnail boots.

In his last letter to England Wilson wrote: "Man proposes and God disposes, though in my case I think he did both. I have the distinct feeling of knowing that I shall return; though if things turn out otherwise I've at least had some kick out of life. And if I had my life to live over again, I wouldn't wish it any other way."

And so, in the very early morning of March 21st, 1934, Maurice Wilson, in his elaborate disguise, slipped quietly out of Darjeeling on the last stage of his journey of no return.

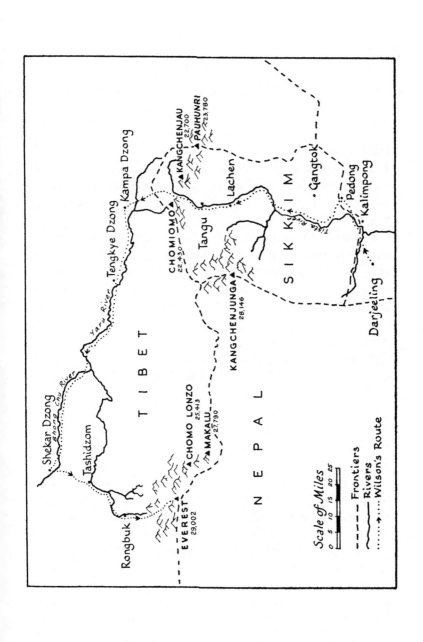

CHAPTER SEVEN

ACROSS THE ROOF OF THE WORLD

Wilson spent the last hours of March 20th packing his few items of equipment, and at 11 p.m. a friend whom he had taken into his confidence over the expedition's plans, came and sewed up his kitbags and disguised them as sacks of wheat. At midnight all was ready for his lone assault to begin.

It had been arranged that Tewang and Rinzing should leave separately and well in advance; this was to lessen the chances of four men travelling together being spotted by the authorities. A meeting place had been fixed in the forest some twenty miles beyond Darjeeling, and here the party were to reassemble at noon.

So it was, that soon after midnight Wilson, disguised as a Tibetan priest, slipped out of his lodgings by a back staircase, and made for his secret rendezvous with Tsering.

The Sherpa arrived on time, and together the two of them picked their way through the back streets of the town. There was an almost full moon and stars sparkled brightly in the clear metallic sky. The light indeed was too strong for Wilson's liking; he feared that his height—six-foot-one—would give him away; and to camouflage this he shuffled along with half-bent knees. Both men were relieved when they left the town behind and began to head down the narrow road toward the Tista Valley.

Just as dawn was breaking they saw, coming toward them, a single policeman.

It was too late for them to hide without arousing his suspicion; so Wilson opened up his umbrella to help his disguise and they walked boldly towards him; Tsering exchanged greetings with the policeman and they passed safely by.

Wilson was shaken. Another time, he told himself, they might not escape so easily.

They decided to leave the road and travel roughly parallel to it, some half-mile to the north-west. The going here was comparatively easy—through open woodland of fir, oak and beech, rather like the Shropshire hills. They reached their rendezvous at 11 a.m. The others had not yet arrived; so while Wilson remained in the forest Tsering went to search for them. After about half an hour he saw the two Sherpas, together with the expedition's single pony, stretched out by the side of the road; they were, it seemed, sleeping off the effects of having celebrated the night before.

Wilson was indignant; but the midday meal soon put him in a happier frame of mind. He hadn't eaten for twenty-four hours, since he had chosen, at this inopportune moment, to embark on one of his semi-fasts. Even now all he had was a large slice of bread and two mugs of steaming tea. But at least this meagre ration restored his good temper.

The party from now on kept to their original plan; resting through the day and travelling only by night.

The route they planned to follow was quite different from that used by Ruttledge the year before. Ruttledge had taken a wide detour along the Chumbi Valley, leaving the main Himalayan peaks—except Chomo Lhari—to the west. Wilson planned to use a shorter but more difficult route, following the Tista Valley almost to its source among the foothills of Kangchenjau. This route wound its way among the heart of the great Himalayan peaks. Kangchenjunga rose some twenty miles to the west; Pauhunri and Kangchenjau less than half that distance to the east; while the shoulder of Chomiomo (22,400 feet) would have to be actually traversed. It was an exacting route to be chosen by a man with no mountaineering experience; and yet Wilson planned to cover a fair part of it by night.

But his decision to avoid travelling during the day was justified that very first evening.

They had started off at dusk, a little after 7 p.m., and for several hours made good progress. Then a little before midnight they again ran into a police patrol. This time they had more warning; and Wilson, deciding not to trust his disguise, took prompt evasive action. He flung himself into a deep ditch, which he soon found to his cost was half-full of water and overgrown with nettles. As at last the patrol disappeared, it was a very sore and bedraggled Tibetan priest who scrambled out of his hiding place; and his language was far from priest-like!

For a couple of days Wilson and the Sherpas followed the lower reaches of the broad Tista Valley, leading roughly north-north-east. The valley, near Darjeeling, is only some thousand feet above sea-level, and its climate, Wilson found, was almost tropical; the air was warm and humid, and giant ferns, orchids and vines grew close-packed in luxuriant profusion. And, of course, there were the leeches.

After Kalimpong, which on the 22nd the party by-passed to the west, the valley began to climb rapidly, and the road soon degenerated into a narrow precipitous mule track. The tropical forest was left behind now, and the party came into more open country; alders and oaks rose in little copses among belts of tall bamboo, and the white dhatura hedges gleamed ghost-like in the bright light of the moon.

Near Pedong they crossed the India-Sikkim frontier. They crept through undetected as the sun rose over the eastern peaks, and lay up for the rest of the day in a thick belt of bamboo.

Soon they evolved a routine for each day's travelling. At dusk Tewang and Rinzing and the heavily-laden pony would break camp and push off up the valley. An hour later Wilson and Tsering would follow them. Each would travel independently during the night, covering some fifteen or eighteen miles before they again pitched camp well before dawn. Tewang and Rinzing would have the tents set up and a meal cooked by the time Wilson arrived; and here the party would sleep and rest until once again darkness began to fall.

A couple of times the Sherpas had to leave Wilson and go into a nearby village for food. When they did this they invariably took care to spread the news that their master was a deaf-and-dumb priest, and also a very sick man. This kept the visitors down to a minimum.

On March 23rd they passed Gangtok, and from now on the valley began to climb due north and very steeply. The going became far harder. In a couple of days they climbed from five thousand to twelve thousand feet.

Rapidly the bamboos thinned and the oak and fir became stunted and finally died away; the slopes became steeper, on a larger scale, and were now covered with outcrops of stone and thin wiry grass. The wind began to strengthen and it became very cold at night.

On March 24th they covered sixteen miles in seven-and-a-half hours; good progress for climbing along an ill-defined track, which in Wilson's words, was like "a reversing spiral staircase". Once in the darkness their pony missed its footing, and slithered almost to the edge of a five-hundred-foot precipice; once they had to ford an ice-cold mountain stream, with the water swirling fast up to their armpits; and once they were caught, at the top of a small pass, in a minor blizzard of sleet—stinging rain and hard-packed granules of snow. Wilson seemed to thrive on discomfort. That night he wrote in his diary: "Party marvellous, couldn't wish for better; all very happy." He went on to note that the few houses they passed "had lights burning in them all night . . . to keep away the spirits."

The next night they passed through a camp of coolie labourers, engaged in carrying parts of an electric cable to Lhasa, several hundred miles to the north. They heard the soft mournful chant of the coolies' singing, echo for a brief moment, then vanish into the silence of the vast Himalayan foothills.

It was on March 27th that they crossed their first patch of snow, at the top of a 13,000-foot pass, a little to the east of Kangchenjunga. From now on the snow was never very far away; and at night the cold of the Himalayan peaks came stealing round their two Meade-type tents.

But the days were hot. A slightly haloed sun blazed out of the cloudless sky; its rays, in the clear air, were surprisingly powerful, and soon Wilson's face was tanned to a shade of deep mahogany. On days when there were many people about Wilson spent much of the time keeping under cover in his tent. The heat, the airlessness and the flies were some-times almost more than he could bear. "Looking forward," he wrote, "to getting over the border and into Tibet. I prefer brigands to staying inside all day." He had one or two anxious moments; especially when one Tibetan refused to be put off by the Sherpas and insisted on seeing "the priest". Wilson received him with his Bhutia cap pulled well down and his earflaps in position. He gave the man some whole-wheat bread—a month old—and eventually the Tibetan went away, apparently in the best of tempers.

The Sherpas were proving their value. Tewang was a reliable guide, Rinzing an excellent cook, and Tsering for most of the time proved an ideal companion. Only when they camped near an inn did Wilson have any trouble; then the three Sherpas would return at dusk, bleary-eyed and bad-tempered and demanding a chit for "baksheesh" in case Wilson failed to return!

As they neared the Tibetan border they met fewer people, and Wilson was able on several afternoons to lie out in the open and admire his surroundings—and they were indeed worthy of admiration. In its upper reaches the Tista River flows through a number of magnificent steep-sided gorges. Here, sheltered from the wind, they would pitch their camp, often in a setting of extreme beauty. Spring flowers were nosing their way out of the thawing earth, and soon the valley would be bright with cowslips and poppies, primula and rhododendron. The river was full—but not in flood—and ice-cold from the snows of Kangchenjunga; it flowed fast, racing white and frothing among the grey slab-sided boul-ders, and every now and then cascading in showers of spray over thirty- to forty-foot waterfalls. Larch and pine clung precariously to the hillside, and towering high over the valley-wall rose the magnificent snow-covered massifs of some of the highest mountains in the world: Kangchenjunga and Chomiomo, Kangchenjau and Pauhunri.

Hardly ever was the serenity of the scene broken by approaching travellers, and on these occasions Wilson feigned sleep and was never troubled.

Soon they by-passed Tangu—site of the highest dak-bungalow in Sikkim. Then they began to pass through small deserted villages, whose inhabitants had not yet returned from wintering in the southern lowlands. At last the Tista Valley began to open out and climb more steeply, and soon Wilson and the Sherpas were scrambling over barren wind-swept slopes at a height of 15,000 feet. They were nearing Kongra La, on the borders of Tibet, and now the snow began to lie in little drifts up to six feet deep.

They gave up travelling by night, and on Wilson's last day in Sikkim the party rose at seven-thirty and after breakfast climbed solidly for five hours. At a little after noon they crossed into Tibet.

*   *   *

It was a magnificent scene that opened out before them; a new world of limitless horizons, very different from the closed-in foothills of Sikkim. To west, north and east lay a magnificent panorama of vast brown and purple hills streaked and capped with snow of a dazzling white. Every outline was sharp-cut, knifing into the thin, bitterly cold air; and all around them great snow-plumed peaks rose in majestic grandeur out of the roof of the world.

Wilson was jubilant. "Now in forbidden Tibet," he wrote, "and feel like sending Government a wire: 'Told you so.'"

But almost at once, within an hour of their setting foot in Tibet, a little incident is recorded in Wilson's diary: an incident that apparently passed almost unnoticed, but which might have served as a presage of the future.

The water for their tea took over an hour to boil. And that night there were thirty-seven degrees of frost.

Their mode of travelling was now completely changed. Gone was the wariness which Wilson had up to now displayed; he discarded his disguise and travelled openly by day—though he still preferred to avoid the few villages they came to, camping always on their outskirts. Secrecy was replaced by speed. That first day they travelled nearly thirty miles over the high Tibetan plateau—an almost incredible feat, albeit a very foolish one. Hour after hour they plodded steadily on; from out of the north-west a chilling wind swept across the snow-sprinkled plateau and above them hung a vast orange ball, the sun, whose rays were burning in the cold rarefied air. By the time they camped for the night all four men and the pony were completely exhausted. The evening meal quickly restored Wilson's spirits, but the night brought him little rest. He suffered from a dull, nagging headache and slept poorly; nor was this surprising, for in a single day they had covered twenty-eight to thirty miles, and traversed a 17,000-foot pass. Without doubt they were climbing too fast for Wilson to become properly acclimatized.

They had hoped to reach Kampa Dzong the next day, and from there head westward along the Yaru Valley; but it became obvious during the night that Wilson could not keep up the pace he had so rashly set. And so on Sunday, April 1st, they rested. Both Wilson and the pony were in poor shape, the former with head and eyes aching, and the latter with sores. The Sherpas, on the other hand, were going well, and spent the day cutting up and cooking goat's meat which they bought from a nearby village. On the night of April 1st and 2nd Wilson again slept badly, but he insisted the next morning that he was well enough to push on. His diary, written up early on the morning of April 2nd reads: "Time flying. Should be at Everest in ten or twelve

Everest from Camp II.
This photograph was taken by the 1935 Reconnaissance Expedition,
which found Wilson's body)

The East Rongbuk Glacier

days now. Spent night at 15,800 feet. Didn't sleep much—
in bed too early perhaps on top of meal. Dusty and blowing
all night."

Sun-up that morning found them on the move again.
They struggled for two-and-a-half hours against the rising
wind before they camped for breakfast; and just before noon
they forded a swift-flowing branch of the Yaru River. Then
they scrambled over another 17,000-foot pass before dropping again into a shallow valley. The wind was paralyzing
but the sun still kept its warmth.

The pony began to prove troublesome. Wilson thought
that it regarded dry straw on the Tibetan plateau a poor
exchange for the succulent greenery of Sikkim. Be that as it
may, in a particularly windswept traverse it bolted, and
headed back for the Tista Valley. The four men gave immediate chase, but it was over a mile before they caught and
tethered the truant and led him back in disgrace.

They camped that night on the edge of a small village.
Tsering went as usual to collect their provisions and returned an hour later with eggs, meal, butter, meat and a
large handful of chillies. The latter, he said, would alleviate
the headaches from which the whole party was now suffering.
The three porters chewed them assiduously, but Wilson
looked on them with scorn. "Headache?" he grunted.
"Haven't noticed one myself!" But this his diary refutes.

Wilson's diary, which was found later on his body at the
approaches to North Col, was a small green booklet—hardly
larger than a pocket-book—which he had bought at Darjeeling a few days before he left. On its binding were the
words, "Present Time Book", and "Made in Japan". Soon
its small coarse-grained pages became filled with the Yorkshireman's strong though spidery writing. He had no-one
as his confidant, and we might have expected him to write
occasionally of the ideals that had brought him so near to
Everest. But this, disappointingly, he never does; and the
diary provides only a somewhat prosaic day-to-day commen-
tary on his routine existence.

On April 2nd, for example, he writes: "Having some real cow's milk this evening, and Tsering is making an omelet. Another two days should see us drop into a more fertile valley, out of the rock and sand. Will be good to see some greenery again. The boys (Sherpas) are already talking about what we are going to do on our way back. It is lovely to have everyone so optimistic. . . . They (the Sherpas) are just having their evening meal; one of them is cutting up the meat that they cooked yesterday, while the others make dough out of a coarse flour and Tibetan tea, which is kneaded together in a goatskin bag. . . . Had bit of a head this evening: too much sun I think."

The next couple of days proved a nightmare—a nightmare of cold and pain, driving sand and utter exhaustion and, above all, of the screaming fury of a relentless northwest wind.

On April 3rd they made a late start, and almost at once, as they struggled over the snow-coated plateau, they ran into a blizzard of driving sleet and whipped-up sand. They covered half-a-mile in three hours. Then once again the pony bolted; and once again they caught it and then drove themselves on. They rested two hours for lunch, in the half-shelter of a great slab of rock, then they pushed forward.

As they climbed an unusually steep slope the wind rose to gale force and they had to hurl themselves against a stinging, almost blinding wall of sand and snow which the wind tore up and drove almost horizontally across the level plain. Within a few minutes their clothes were caked with sand and melting snow, and their eyes smarted as though they had been pricked by red-hot needles. Then after two hours came a little relief; they dropped into a shallow valley, and just before sunset the wind began to die away. But once it was dark and the encircling rim of peaks glinted sharp-outlined against the night sky, it became very cold. At midnight Wilson's thermometer registered forty-eight degrees of frost; the cold was like that of interstellar space.

April 4th dawned, still bitterly cold, but fine; and it

seemed at first as though the wind itself had been frozen into stillness. But the lull was short-lived. As Wilson and the Sherpas climbed out of the valley the wind once again came screaming down at them, tearing madly out of the west-north-west, directly into their faces. Dark masses of snow and sand, ripped off the plateau, darkened out the sun; and they could only crawl slowly and half-blindly forward into the teeth of the raging inferno. They inched painfully towards a narrow cleft in the plateau. When they reached it the wind was tremendous, and they could only crawl forward on hands and knees. But they had passed the worst now; and at last Tsering, speechless with exhaustion, pointed to a nearby ridge which fringed the Yaru Valley. Once over that, Wilson gathered, they would find at least a trace of shelter. Making a supreme effort they staggered towards the ridge. It took them an hour to cover three hundred yards, but at last they scrambled down into the wide U-shaped valley with its merciful promise of shelter. And the lower they descended the less furious the wind became, until by evening they were able to approach Kampa Dzong in comparative comfort.

Most of the pre-war expeditions to Everest passed through Kampa Dzong, and much has been written of its austere but impressive beauty. The monastic buildings cling to a precipitous rock which rises for some five hundred feet from the floor of the Yaru Valley. The rounded towers spiral up, one above the other, connected by massive walls; and from the upper roof there unfolds a magnificent panorama of range after range of mighty snow-clad peaks: Pauhunri, Kangchenjau, and Chomiomo in the south-east; Kangchen-junga and Jonsong in the south-west; and far away on the western horizon, the graceful Makalu and a vast snowy triangle that could only be Mount Everest.

Wilson spent the night camped just outside the monastery, then pressed on up the sheltered Yaru Valley. He made good progress for a couple of days, passing Tengkye Dzong, then crossing the Tengkye La and descending into a tributary of the Yaru. It was an exacting journey, but the magnificent scenery was some compensation.

Considering the speed at which they were now travelling Wilson was remarkably fit. Obviously he could not have been properly acclimatized, yet apart from a slight nagging headache and a difficulty in dropping off to sleep, he felt well, and was climbing as comfortably as the Sherpas.

In the last week of his trek to Everest he averaged some twenty miles a day, and this at a height of over 15,000 feet. His diary, however, makes no mention of any difficulties, hardships, or discomforts. It is full of somewhat trivial entries.

"*Friday, April 6th.* Started early and had breakfast *en route.* Were just breaking camp when whole family came up: so happy. Made use of our fire and remnants of fuel . . . Camped for night in lovely spot away from wind. Tsering gone for eggs, etc. . . . (later). No eggs so had uncooked oats and chupatties."

"*Saturday, April 7th.* Had long trek today and camped at 3.30. More of interest now, as seem to be getting more into wilds. Sky cloudy for first time. Feel exceedingly fit. Haven't had drink all day, but just gone off the rails with a pot of tea! Fairly wide river to cross tomorrow, so all look like having to strip. Wonder what's happening in Darjeeling?"

"*Sunday, April 8th.* Three or four days hence, shall be seeing Everest. Had early meal, though didn't make start till later. Had to ford river, then very long trek and camped at 2.30. . . . Everybody optimistic and talking of what we will do on way back."

"*Monday, April 9th.* Had very good trek over rougher country than usual. Tsering gone to buy food for remainder of trip. . . . Last 3 nights been sheltered and surprisingly warm at 15,000 feet. . . . Now time is flying. Cannot speak much to boys (Sherpas) so am looking forward to a good nag. Just as well I'm used to my own company."

"*Tuesday, April 10th.* Sixteen years since I went into line in France. . . . No more tea, no more honey, so shall box on without them."

"*Wednesday, April* 11*th.* Shall be in sight of Everest to-morrow. Camped about 12.30 and ate early. Had bit of a head today."

"*Thursday, April* 12*th.* Saw Everest this morning from 17,000 feet ridge. Looked magnificent. Eastern half in snow plume. Tsering says I've come at right time of year for scenery as later mountain is always in cloud. Two nights from now shall be at Rongbuk where I hope to fast for a couple of days to get ready for the big climb. Am already planning for future after the event. I *must* win."

All this while Wilson had been heading roughly west along the Bhong Chu River, a tributary of the Yaru. The route he followed was more arduous than hazardous, though at a height of some 15,000 feet the going was never exactly easy. It was bleak, desolate country—"looks to me," wrote Wilson, "like the mountains of the moon." As far as the eye could see, the vast Tibetan plateau lay spread out before them, dotted with isolated stony hills, conical in shape and quite devoid of any vegetation. Near Kyishong they had to scramble over an 18,000-foot ridge, and from the top they looked across a magnificent landscape of valley and snow-capped mountain, to where Shekar Dzong soared out of a stretch of level plain on its fantastic pyramid of rock.

A couple of hours later Wilson was helping his Sherpas pitch camp in the shadow of the famous monastery.

Had the Western geographers known of Shekar Dzong they would certainly have ranked it as one of the seven wonders of the world. Its name, which means "white glass" is unusually descriptive. The actual village of white-stone houses lies clustered round the base of a towering mass of rock; and half-way up the rock, built with amazing artistry along a series of narrow winding ledges, there rise the glisten-ing walls of two great monasteries. Above them rises the Dzong itself, and on the very highest pinnacle some thousand feet above the plain, is a single look-out post; a post with what are surely the most magnificent views in the world. Even more than at Kampa Dzong, here was a fairy-story setting, a place of almost ethereal enchantment.

Wilson saw only a couple of the monasteries' four hundred monks, for at dawn the next day—April 13th—he and the Sherpas broke camp and headed south, over the Pang La toward Tashidzom and Rongbuk. That day they covered well over twenty-five miles, camping only when dark began to fall.

They had just set up their tents and Tsering was tending an unwilling fire with his primitive bellows, when a group of wandering musicians unexpectedly appeared. They played a repetitious, and to Wilson's way of thinking, somewhat mournful dirge; but their voices were soft and melodious, and he could have listened to them happily for hours. The Sherpas, however, thought they were annoying him, and persuaded them on their way with a little money and some very ancient *tampsa*; "a pity," wrote Wilson; "they were so quaint with their thin one-stringed instruments."

That night he realized he was on the threshold of the last stage of his amazing quest, a quest that had already brought him to a height of 16,000 feet and a third of the way round the world. To-morrow, at the final bend of the Rongbuk Valley he would come face to face with Everest. "Maybe," he wrote in his diary, "in less than five weeks the world will be on fire."

The next day, April 14th, the party set out early and soon covered the twelve miles to the head of the Rongbuk Valley. At first they climbed along the shelves of what looked like gigantic moraines, but which were in fact age-old river terraces. Then the valley narrowed; the hills closed in around them, and soon a south wind, ice-cold from the snows of Everest, began to drive in erratic stinging gusts into their faces.

Gradually the thin grass disappeared. From now on boulder and scree, moraine and glacier, blue ice and snow were all of this world that Wilson was ever to see.

It was a world of vast proportions that he came to that April morning; a world of almost lunar desolation; and, above all, a world when darkness brought each night the most appalling cold—it is hard for a man to be brave when he is alone and everlastingly cold.

Wilson's first sight, at close range, of Everest was spectacular. At one moment he and the Sherpas were walking along a rough snow-covered track, in a valley which seemed to lead to nowhere in particular; then suddenly a corner was turned and there lay the monastery, its massive walls utterly dwarfed by the magnificent mountain which rose less than twenty miles distant at the head of the Rongbuk Valley. Everest, snow-plumed, and in all her rugged beauty filled the entire scene. In the foreground the long Rongbuk Glacier wound its way upward to impregnable cliffs of grey rock and dark-blue ice, while beyond these rose far into the sky the majestic mass of her upper slopes sweeping toward the summit.

Everest—Chomolungma, the Goddess Mother of the World—lay waiting.

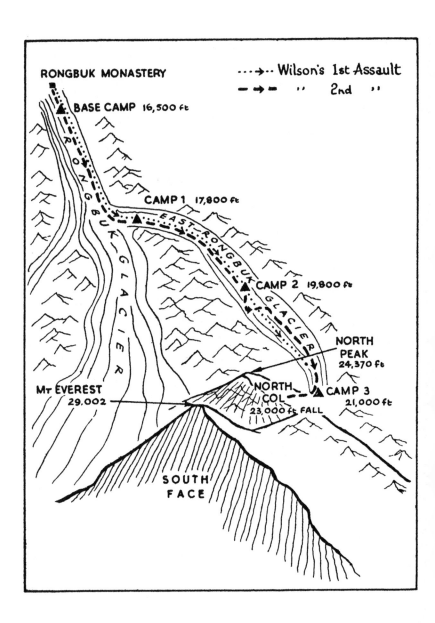

CHAPTER EIGHT

THE FIRST ASSAULT

Wᴵˡˢᴼᴺ'ˢ ᴶᴼᵁᴿᴺᴱʸ to the foot of Everest was an incredible
achievement. When he left England he had been a pilot
with less than two months' flying experience; yet he had
confounded the experts by safely piloting his plane for more
than five thousand miles over difficult country and in the face
of determined efforts to stop him. He was a man of no mountaineering ability; yet he had made his way for three hundred
miles across Sikkim and Tibet—the roof of the world—travelling often by night; and, what is more, he had covered the
distance in only twenty-five days—ten days less than the
time taken by the Ruttledge Expedition of 1933. In one way
of course there was no particular merit in Wilson having
made such fast time; the Ruttledge Expedition were travelling with deliberate slowness to help their acclimatization;
but on the other hand mountaineers themselves afterwards
spoke of Wilson's trek to Everest in such terms as "an extraordinary achievement", "a first-class effort", and even as "a
minor epic of endurance".

So far Wilson had overcome every obstacle that had
faced him, and people began to wonder if he might not after
all, overcome the final obstacle, Everest herself. The Press
got to hear of his "escape" from Darjeeling; rumours began
to spread of his arrival on Everest's lower slopes; and soon
the world was waiting eagerly for news of the amazing man
who believed he could climb alone to the summit of the
highest mountain on earth.

Expert opinion condemned his assault as "an elaborate
form of suicide". But then expert opinion had been equally
scathing about his attempted flight to India; and without
doubt the vast majority of people, all over the world, wished
Wilson well and probably gave him an outside chance of

success. But in actual fact he had—barring a miracle—no chance at all. The scales were weighted imponderably against him. A very fair assessment of the whole position appeared in the Press that spring:

"While one cannot but admire the pluck of Captain Maurice Wilson," the article ran, "in attempting to climb Mount Everest alone, his whole project and his training methods in particular seem to have been ill-judged. It is said that he has been fasting for five months and accustoming himself to a diet of figs, dates and cereals. This will be just about as useful to him in his present venture as it would be if he were intending to swim the Atlantic. The experience of various expeditions which have already attempted the ascent prove beyond question that a large organization is essential if the mountain is to be conquered. Mr. George Mallory told me after the first expedition—he was killed on the second—that in his view Everest could be climbed only if the attack were organized with the same thoroughness as a wartime offensive.

"The physical discomfort, compounded of intense cold, perpetual blizzard and the rarefied air, produce on the mountain a feeling of depression and hopelessness. This can only be counteracted by human companionship, shelter and proper food. Apart from these considerations, Everest presents considerable technical climbing difficulties."

The last point was the reef on which Wilson's hopes were predestined to founder. He might be fit enough to withstand the cold, strong enough to force his way upwards through the blizzards and rarefied air, brave and determined enough to overcome the fear, loneliness and depression; but still he would never climb Mount Everest. For he lacked the technical climbing ability that was essential to success.

The tragedy—and the grandeur—of Wilson's story springs from the fact that in the last few weeks of his life he must surely have known that he could never succeed.

And yet he still went on.

Nor was this going-on a matter, for Wilson, of blind

stupidity or obstinate defiance. It was a matter of faith. For the end of his story was in the germ of its beginning; and as in a pure unclouded faith his quest had begun so in a faith still immaculate it drew to its inevitable end. Wilson believed that God, who had told Simon Peter to walk the waters of Galilee, would guide his feet up the glaciers and ice walls of Mount Everest. And even when at the end it must have seemed that God had utterly deserted him, when he felt himself day after day slowly dying among the seracs and crevasses that guard the North Col, yet still he refused to give up, still he struggled on towards his unachievable ideal. "Faith," he wrote in one of the rare reflective passages in his diary, "is not faith that wavers when its prayers remain unanswered."

Yet though Wilson hoped, as one unkind critic put it, "to climb Everest on faith and figs," his attempt was not in some ways ill-conceived, nor was it, in the light of his mountaineering ability, inexpertly carried out. There are not, after all, many men who have climbed to 22,000 feet, alone.

His timing at least could hardly have been bettered. In 1933 the Ruttledge Expedition had arrived at Rongbuk on Monday, April 17th, which was considered the ideal date for an early start on the actual climb. In 1934 Wilson arrived on Saturday, April 14th, and started his ascent two days later.

His equipment—as regards clothing—was eminently sensible: light-weight, but warm and windproof. His route followed what was then regarded as the only possible way to the summit: along the subsidiary East Rongbuk Glacier, thence via the North Col on to the north-west arete of the final pyramid. If his provisions seemed unorthodox, it should be remembered that a vegetarian diet had brought him to 16,000 feet in fine physical condition; also that fasting formed an integral part of his "training". Only in one respect did his preparations fall short of what would obviously be needed. Of all those items of climbing equipment so indispensable to the mountaineer, he took with him only a single length of rope and one ice axe. Neither of these could he use with any semblance of efficiency.

It was in gathering together this scanty equipment, and in prayer and fasting, that Wilson passed his last two days at Rongbuk.

At first, the monastery seems to have made little impression on him. He comments briefly on its beauty of setting, then adds, in the same sentence, "but the people in it are filthy—men, women and children too." This opinion, however, he was to change when the next day—April 15th—he was invited to call on the Head Lama.

This visit came as a direct result of Wilson having asked if he could make use of the stores left in the Monastery by Ruttledge's Expedition. He had decided that he would tell the Lamas he was a member of this expedition, who had now returned for a reconnaissance climb; and this decision he at first adhered to. But the Lamas were discerning men. Each member of the Ruttledge Expedition had been presented personally to the Head Lama, who knew very well that Wilson was a stranger. Nevertheless his request was granted; and Wilson spent the morning sorting out those items of equipment that he thought might be useful to him. Strangely enough it never seemed to occur to him that he was breaking the Eighth Commandment, and he rummaged happily among the stores helping himself to whatever he fancied. His most important acquisitions were an improved-type Meade tent, a Tommy cooker and a collapsible lantern.

That afternoon he and his three Sherpas were received in audience by the Head Lama.

The head of the Rongbuk Monastery is a man of great influence and high reputation, and his blessing is eagerly sought by Tibetans and Sherpas alike; nor would the European members of an expedition be entirely happy about attempting Everest from Rongbuk, without first being received in audience and reciting to the Head Lama the mystic words, "OM MANI PADME HUM", (Hail, the jewel in the lotus),

and being touched with his sacred *dorje*. His meeting with
Wilson was a moving occasion. The latter had spent several
hours in making himself presentable—enjoying his first
bath for many weeks and tidying up his best European
clothes. Then a little before dark he and Tsering, Tewang
and Rinzing were escorted through the long stone corridors
of Rongbuk Monastery, and up the rickety step-ladder,
which seemed to serve as stairs, until in a little room near the
top of the building they were presented to the Lama.

It was a plain wooden room he received them in, with
windows of real glass—a great rarity in Tibet. A handful of
the more senior monks and an interpreter were also present.

The Lama himself was a man, some seventy years old, of
great dignity, whose power in the monastery was absolute.
But in spite of his position he proved himself a very human
and indeed jovial character. Through their interpreter he
and Wilson talked for over half an hour, Wilson relating his
travels round the world, and the Lama telling him of the
monastic life at Rongbuk. The two men were obviously
attracted to each other. Wilson wrote in his diary, "I told
him I had travelled the world over and never felt so happy
in anybody's company before"; while the Lama told members of later expeditions how impressed he had been with
Wilson's courage and determination and how his death had
been a deep and almost personal grief to him. At the end of
the audience the Lama invited Wilson to eat with him on his
return from Everest.

"I shall be delighted," Wilson said.

He then moved back and motioned Tsering to present the
Lama with his gift. As the Sherpa stepped forward with an
openwork scarf and three rupees Wilson could hardly hide
his smile. "Lucky he didn't know," he wrote, "that it was a
scarf I'd often wiped my knife on after spreading the mar-
garine!"

As a return gift the Lama offered Wilson a huge bowl of
meal and half a fried goat. He then gave him and the
Sherpas his blessing, touching their heads with his *dorje* while

they recited the words, "OM MANI PADME HUM." Wilson's pronunciation failed him, and the Lama chuckled with delight and tapped him reprovingly with the *dorje*.

Afterwards the monks crowded round Wilson and readily agreed to watch his progress up the mountain; he would, he said, heliograph them with a small mirror which he had bought specially for this purpose. And when the presentations were all over Wilson asked for permission to photograph both the Lama and his quarters, and this was cheerfully given. The quarters were not the austere cells Wilson had half expected; but rooms of great beauty with wonderful decorations in the most subtle and delicate colours.

That evening Wilson sat in his tent making a few last entries in his diary. Tomorrow the climax of his lone assault would begin. He was very matter-of-fact about the whole business. "Everest looked wonderful this p.m.," he wrote. "Am starting the job tomorrow; only another thirteen thousand feet to go! Having a darned good bath and rub down now, before getting into my full kit tomorrow. Boys all looking forward to my getting it over quickly; they've been wonderful throughout."

And late that night there occurred a little incident which showed that his opinion of the Sherpas was reciprocated.

It was about nine o'clock, and Wilson had just finished checking his equipment. He found he was short of candles and called out to Tsering, in his nearby tent, to knock up the monastery and see if he could get some. Before he left, Tsering, as a sign of respect, gave Wilson a sweeping salaam, touching the ground with his forehead. Wilson realized the significance of this gesture from a man he had always treated as an equal, and was embarrassed. He told him to rise, and when ten minutes later he came back with the candles, he shook him by the hand and thanked him for his loyalty and devotion.

Then at 9.30 p.m. he settled down for the night, almost the last night of comfort and security he was ever to enjoy.

*　　　*　　　*

He rose at dawn, dressed carefully, shouldered his forty-five pounds of kit and set out along the gently sloping Rong-buk Valley. As he left, the low chanting of the monastery's three hundred monks was rising and falling into the still morning air. He liked to think that they were praying for his success. It was a perfect day, with the merest trace of a south-west breeze; and the highest mountain in the world rose in all her majesty less than a dozen miles away.

As he climbed slowly towards her he could pick out the famous route, pioneered by Howard-Bury, immortalized by Irvine and Mallory, and used with such determination less than a year ago by Ruttledge. Dead ahead the winding ribbon of the Rongbuk Glacier, with its seracs and pinnacles of fluted ice, soared upwards to culminate in the precipitous cliffs of the north face, deemed unclimbable by Mallory; while to his left wound the curve of the subsidiary East Rongbuk Glacier, along which his path lay. This glacier rose at a comparatively gentle gradient from 17,500 feet to a little over 21,000 feet where it culminated in the great ice-fall guarding the approaches to North Col. Above the col was the North (or Changtse) Peak, and only a little behind it and to its right rose the final pyramid of the summit.

At first the going was easy, and soon Wilson passed the site of Ruttledge's Base Camp at some 16,500 feet. His load—forty-five pounds—was a heavy one, even for a Sherpa, at this height, but Wilson was remarkably fit and strong, and that first day he made excellent progress. Every now and then he paused to check his height recorder, and he must have felt well satisfied as he steadily gained height and the distance between him and the summit decreased hour by hour.

Mid-day saw him plodding steadily on towards the dull grey moraines, with the heat of the sun sending rivulets of perspiration trickling from under his arms. He began to wish he had left off some of his four layers of woollen underwear. As he climbed higher the summit of Everest gradually disappeared behind the massive wall of the North Peak. Wilson was sorry about this. "I like," he wrote that night in his diary, "to see where I'm going."

He had climbed eight miles and well over 1,200 feet by 3 p.m. and decided he would pitch camp now, in good time, and while the sun's rays would still warm him as he set about erecting his tent. He eventually found a level area of ground, where a forty-foot high moraine bank afforded first-class shelter. It was a somewhat desolate site, but a good one nevertheless, and within half an hour of his arrival Wilson had the tent up, his stores out and was brewing tea on his Tommy cooker. He was at 17,600 feet, some three-quarters of a mile from Ruttledge's Camp I.

The weather remained on its best behaviour; a perfect day was followed by a perfect night. Wilson snuggled into his sleeping bag and almost at once fell into a deep refreshing sleep. There was scarcely a murmur from the winds that could so easily make even the lower slopes of Everest a screaming inferno; and it was, in the shelter of the moraine, surprisingly warm. Once in his sleeping bag Wilson wrote up his diary. "April 16th, Mon. We're off and have got a good start as I'm only three-quarters of a mile from Camp I. Hope to get to Camp II to-morrow, then will be happy. Am carrying terrific load, greater I should imagine than any Sherpa was allowed to carry. Am delighted that have been able to bring such a lot; have not sacrificed essential comforts to lightness. It's early, but am just about to roll off to sleep, as was too damned cold to get much last night at Rongbuk. Weather perfect; hardly a breeze."

That night Wilson surely dreamed of success; but the very next day his self-satisfaction was to turn to something akin to despair as hour after hour he was to struggle unavailingly along the desolate wilderness of the East Rongbuk Glacier.

Tuesday, April 17th, again dawned fine, with only a light south-east breeze blowing in fits and starts down the glaciers. Wilson wanted to make an early start and was up at first light; much to his annoyance, however, it took him the best part of three-quarters of an hour to warm up his somewhat

inadequate breakfast and lukewarm oats. It was eight
o'clock before he had eaten, packed up his equipment and
started off. After about an hour he reached the division of
the Rongbuk and East Rongbuk Glaciers, and almost at
once came across the remains of Ruttledge's Camp I at
17,800 feet.

It was a welcome find, confirming he was on exactly the
right route, and here he rested awhile to admire what was
perhaps the finest view in the world.

To his left, forming the north wall of the East Rongbuk
Glacier, rose a series of vast unclimbable spires, soaring to a
height of over 23,000 feet; they were a dull rusty red, like
certain of the Dolomites or some of the Cuillin of Skye.
Ahead rose the fantastic glacier; its foreground consisting of
low banks of moraine which thrust their grey tongues into
the gleaming ice of the glacier itself. Beyond and above this
foreground, the grey of the moraine disappeared, the seracs
and pinnacles of ice—some of them a hundred feet in height,
crowded closely together, until they merged into one vast
tumbling ice-green sea, that rose in wave after fantastic wave
to the foot of the North Col. While a little to the right,
across miles of grey-green and grey-blue seracs and dark
cliffs rose the massive shoulder of the North Peak.

It was a scene of great beauty and impressive grandeur;
but it can hardly have reassured Wilson, who saw ahead of
him, in the pinnacles and crevasses of the East Rongbuk
Glacier, the first mountaineering problem he had ever met.

Whatever he may have felt, the glacier was there; there
was no way round it, so obviously it would have to be
climbed. He set out along one edge, trying as far as possible
to follow the lead of the moraines. It was arduous rather
than difficult climbing, but Wilson's inexperience led to his
making of it extremely heavy weather. Trying to pick his
way among the towering pinnacles of ice he lost all sense of
direction, and by mid-day was well and truly lost. Snow-
drifts that lay deeply in the moraine troughs slowed him
down to a breathless one-step-at-a-time advance; when he

tried to climb the slopes of the moraine he found himself quickly becoming exhausted as he leapt from one precarious boulder to the next; when he neared the seracs of ice their cracking and obvious instability warned him off. Nevertheless he pushed resolutely on, heading roughly in the right direction, coming often to culs-de-sac and having to retrace his steps, but most of the time slowly gaining height.

It was exhausting work. He found that he had to stop at fairly frequent intervals to regain his breath. He found too that his load was much too heavy, and gradually he reduced it. First he discarded one of his two Tommy cookers—why he ever took more than one remains a complete mystery. Next to go were half his candles, then half his rolls of film. The sun streamed down out of a cloudless sky, and in the troughs between the moraines, where Wilson pushed doggedly on, the air hung motionless and stagnant. He felt incredibly weary and slightly sick. Any mountaineer could have told him that he was suffering from glacier lassitude, and that an hour's rest on higher ground would have afforded at least a temporary relief. But Wilson, in his pathetic ignorance could only push wearily on.

It was no mean achievement for him on this second day to have again climbed some twelve hundred feet before pitching his tent for the night. He was of course disappointed at having failed to reach the site of Camp II, but he had sufficient common sense not to push on after three o'clock in the hope of getting there. For though on the glacier it was still hot well into the afternoon, once the sun sinks behind the North Peak there is an amazing drop in temperature—a fall of anything up to sixty degrees in half-a-dozen hours. It says much for Wilson's fitness and powers of endurance, that the evening meal quickly revived his spirits, and that once again he slept well. But writing up his diary by the light of a couple of candles he sounds, for the first time, a somewhat despondent note. "Apl. 17th, Tues.," the entry runs. "Had a hell of a day on E. Rongbuk Glacier. Been floundering about doing 50 times more work than necessary. Reduced

load 2 times, but only done about ½ distance I had hoped.
. . . Height a bit under 19,000 feet. . . . Looking forward
to getting to Camp III, from which climb really starts. Shall
do utmost get there tomorrow night . . ."

But it was not "tomorrow", nor even the day after, that
Maurice Wilson was to struggle half-dead with exhaustion
into the windswept camp beneath the shadow of North Col.

The next day, April 18th, saw him make another early
start. In spite of his exertions of the day before, he had
apparently slept well and was still feeling perfectly fit. He
began the day somewhat poorly, with another breakfast of
lukewarm tea and tepid oats—he was still, incidentally,
keeping to his unorthodox diet—but by eight o'clock he was
again ploughing doggedly through the snow-filled glacier
troughs. A little after noon the North Peak disappeared behind a veil of cloud, and half an hour later little flurries of
fine powder snow came drifting down the glacier. It became
suddenly colder. Still Wilson pushed on, finding the going
a little easier now; and at four o'clock he struggled, breathless and weary into the site of Camp II, half-way up the
glacier at a height of 19,800 feet. A good hot meal would
have done much to revive him; but either through exhaustion or fanaticism he simply squatted down and munched a
handful of dates and two slices of bread. He was disappointed
at not having reached Camp III, and it came to him that he
now had little chance of reaching the summit on his birthday
—on which he had set his heart. His thoughts were cut short
by a sudden and heavier fall of snow, and as darkness fell he
found himself battling against a terrible weariness which
threatened to steal over him before his tent was set up. He
had, however, sufficient will-power to make camp efficiently
before it was too late. He crawled into his sleeping-bag and
settled down for what turned out to be a cold, miserable
night.

Next dawn, however, saw him up and about and foraging
among the remains of Ruttledge's Camp II. He hoped to
find either food or cigarettes, but all he unearthed was a pair

of crampons. These in actual fact were about the most useful acquisition he could have made; but Wilson failed to realize their usefulness and threw them disappointedly aside. After his stock breakfast of lukewarm tea and oats—which took him an hour-and-a-half to prepare—he again set off up the East Rongbuk Glacier.

After Camp II he found that the character of the going changed radically.

The pinnacles, seracs and crevasses had extended, of course, far below Camp II, but up to now they had been everywhere flanked by great moraines, which had afforded Wilson a broken but reasonably obvious route over the glacier. But the last of these moraines led up to the site of Camp II; above was a vast and continuous sea of tumbled ice, the wave crests being seracs, of anything up to a hundred and fifteen feet in height. Further advance would have been almost impossible, had it not been for the presence of two long furrows which ran, for some mile-and-a-half up the centre of the glacier, before finally petering out on the approaches to the North Col ice-fall.

Had he been an experienced mountaineer Wilson would have realized that his best plan was to scramble up the loose rock flanking the glacier, then cut across to these furrows at right angles and follow them to their head. (This was the route followed by the Ruttledge Expedition.) However, in his ignorance, he chose to head for the furrows directly up the beautiful but extremely difficult face of the glacier; and almost at once he became hopelessly lost in the bewildering maze of ice-blue seracs, masked crevasses and vast cathedrals of delicately fluted ice. The ice, especially in the shade, was hard and slippery: he had no crampons and lacked the skill to cut proper steps.

Soon, to add to his troubles, it began to snow; but he struggled on, hour after hour, following one false lead after another, constantly slipping on the ice, but somehow always managing to avoid the half-hidden crevasses, any one of which could well have ended his fantastic assault. It was three o'clock before he pitched camp. In six hours he had covered three-quarters of a mile and climbed two hundred and fifty feet. His diary is briefly expressive: "April 19th, Thurs. Another hellish day! About an hour after struck camp it started snowing and hasn't stopped yet. Had to camp again only ¾ mile from previous posn. Got dreadful thirst on this damned glacier—don't know why—and am eating good deal of snow and ice. Did bit of reconnaissance before making camp and discovered good route, along trough, for tomorrow. Hope visibility good."

April 20th dawned bitterly cold and deceptively clear. The massive cliffs and ice-falls of the North Col, sharply defined, looked almost close enough to be reached that afternoon. Wilson had somehow managed to sleep well, and he made another early start. "Thank God," he wrote, "for the snow. Having no crampons I might have been unable to scramble down into trough; as it is, snow gives me a foothold." Once in the trough Wilson began to make good progress up the East Rongbuk Glacier. For about an hour he climbed steadily, stamping out his trail along one edge of the trough, where snow had fallen, melted and then refrozen on the hard surface of the ice. But soon an utter and depressing weariness began to creep inexorably over him. He was feeling the effects of glacier lassitude.

This phenomenon is very aptly described by Ruttledge, who experienced it in these very furrows of the East Rongbuk Glacier. "The sole disadvantage," he wrote, "of these troughs is the presence of stagnant air which induces an extraordinary and devitalizing lassitude . . . you might be going well on the open glacier and be congratulating yourself on your fitness. Five minutes later, in the trough, you can hardly place one foot in front of the other, and discover a marvellous appreciation of the ice scenery, which is of course best observed from a seat on some convenient stone."

More and more often, as he plodded slowly up the trough, Wilson found himself stopping to admire the fantastic beauty of the East Rongbuk Glacier.

And what a breath-taking beauty it was! Even colour photography can render no true picture of the subtle, translucent loveliness of the sea of pinnacles and seracs that rose on every side into a sky of the deepest azure blue. White and blue, green and grey, the terraced palaces of ice lay in wide-flung ruin as far as the eye could see; some, solidly-based on vast foundations of ice; others, hanging poised, as if defying gravity, held only by some slender span of semi-transparent snow. And over the whole scene—silence; save for the murmur, far below, of some subterranean glacial stream or the occasional crack of an insecure serac.

For the first part of the day Wilson made good progress, in spite of his fairly frequent halts; but then, once again, it began to snow, this time in vicious little flurries that came sweeping down the glacier-face. He was forced, as the snow eventually increased to a full blizzard, to pitch camp near the head of the trough. He was at about 20,500 feet, only a couple of miles from Camp III.

Wilson was disappointed but—at least at first—philosophical. He had specially wanted to reach Camp III where his Sherpas had told him he would find a ration dump left by the previous expedition: "Was looking forward," he wrote, "to some hot chocolate . . . think I shall have to take a bit more to eat to see if that won't solve this lassitude business. Still I don't feel any real ill effects yet; no hardship in breathing." Nevertheless it was this evening, as he lay alone in his blizzard-swept tent—sleeping higher probably than any other man in the world—that he first began to have doubts about the success of his venture, and gave vent to his feelings in one of the few self-pitying complaints in his whole diary. "If," he wrote, "I had had services of Sherpas like expdns., should have been at Camp IV by now. Think the others had it cushy compared with me."

Wilson, though apparently he did not realize it, was already in a somewhat precarious position. For the whole success of his venture now hung on his reaching Camp III and its supply dump, before his own meagre and inadequate supplies ran out. He had, it is true, still enough food of sorts for several days; but the weather seemed to be deteriorating fast, and he was ill-equipped to lie up in his glacier-trough camp for a long period.

At dawn the next morning he looked hopefully out of his tent, but he saw it was still snowing hard.

And it continued to snow, day after day, with persistent and relentless fury, until Wilson found his store of food had dwindled practically away and the numbing cold had eaten deep into his being and would not be driven away.

Hour after hour, day after day, he sat in his storm-swept tent, at 20,500 feet, listening to the roar of the blizzard that tore and thundered down the glacier. Twice he thought the weather was going to clear; and twice he struck camp and struggled on a few hundred yards, only to be overtaken by another blizzard in which no man in the open could live.

His birthday, April 21st, the day on which he had set his heart on reaching the summit—saw him still 8,500 feet from his goal, snow-bound in the glacier trough. He spent a miserable day. "Apl. 21st, Sat," he wrote, "36 to-day. Wished myself many happy returns. Had hellish cold feet all night. Storm still raging, so am finishing breakfast and shall try to get a little sleep. P.M. off again, but overtaken by another snowstorm and camped early. Eyes bad. Throat dry."

Some time toward the end of the third day of the blizzard Wilson took stock of his situation. He realized that he had three courses open to him. He could push on, into the teeth of the storm, and chance finding Ruttledge's supply dump near Camp III, and risk being able to pitch a sheltered well-stocked camp under the North Col ice fall. He could stay where he was, with food for only a couple of days, and hope that the weather would clear. Or he could retrace his steps, retreating along the path he knew, until he reached the safety of Rongbuk Monastery, where he would lie up and recuperate until the weather cleared; then he could launch another assault on Everest—this time with better stocks of food.

Wilson was rash, stubborn and fanatical; but his aim was to climb Mount Everest, not commit suicide; and he realized that only the last course offered him any chance of success. "Discretion," he wrote, "is better part of valour. No use going on. Eyes terrible and throat dry and v. sore. Even with herculean effort might not make Camp III safely. And what if food is not there? Weather still v. bad. Will start back to-morrow if at all possible. It's the weather that has beaten me—what damned bad luck!"

It was not of course "damned bad luck". It was what Wilson ought to have expected. He had read accounts of previous Everest expeditions, and their experiences ought to have taught him that on the highest mountain in the world there is no such thing as good weather, only varying degrees of bad. Had he been caught higher up the mountain with his pitifully inadequate handful of figs, dates and oats he could hardly have survived to make another attempt.

And as it was, his safe return to Rongbuk can only be described as a near-miracle.

He had to wait more than another twenty-four hours before the weather cleared sufficiently for him to make a start. Then, a little before 3 p.m. on Monday, April 23rd, the snow abruptly stopped; the wind began to die down and a veil of tangled cloud streamed away from the face of the North Peak. Late as it was Wilson struck camp. He left all his surplus equipment—camera, films, extra clothing, etc.— on the edge of the glacier trough. Then, carrying only a skeleton load containing his tent, flea-bag and the last of his rations (barely enough for forty-eight hours) he fled—there is no other word for it—down the glacier. His eyes were red and inflamed; his throat was dry, and he again started to eat the newly fallen snow, which lay in drifts along the trough edge, over three feet thick. The going was not easy; but perhaps fear was his pace-maker, for within a couple of hours he reached the site of Camp II, just as another iso-lated snow squall came sweeping down the glacier. The sun set before his camp was pitched, and as he was tightening the guy-ropes a thin crescent moon swung coldly into the sky above the graceful spire of Makalu. Within a couple of hours the thermometer was registering fifty-four degrees of frost.

It speaks well for Wilson's fitness that he came safely through the night, and even managed to sleep, if only in fits and starts. Four-thirty a.m. saw him trying to warm up his few remaining oats, and well before six he had struck camp and was scrambling and slithering, with more haste than skill, down the East Rongbuk Glacier. The weather was uncertain, but for the moment at least the snow had mercifully stopped.

Once again the going was difficult. Newly fallen snow masked the moraines, whose boulders and screes were now covered with some six or nine inches of clinging whiteness— snow and ice that had partially thawed and then re-frozen. This coating of white disguised the more unstable boulders, yet was not thick enough to secure them; and several times Wilson, jumping from one rock to the next, lost his footing and went tumbling in a minor avalanche of snow and boulder down the steep-sided moraines. Soon he was limping badly, and his left arm—never strong at the best of times—started to ache with a dull, nagging pain.

He decided to avoid the moraine and work his way down, along a thin ribbon of flat-looking ice. But here too he was soon in difficulties. For the ice was uneven in texture, and its apparent flatness a cruel deception. He found when he examined it closely that the ice was in fact extremely rough, being full of little holes and criss-crossed with miniature watercourses; these latter had vertical sides some six to twelve inches high, and were reasonably soft. But the inter- vening knobs and plateaux were, under their thin coating of snow, amazingly hard and smooth; and their colour was far bluer than the usual glacier ice. Here, too, Wilson fre- quently lost his footing, and crashed heavily down on to the smooth, unyielding protuberances. At some risk and con- siderable discomfort he then decided to glissade down some of the gentler gradients. Once he found himself, utterly out of control, sliding straight toward a narrow crevasse which split the glacier slope between two unstable buttresses of ice. He drove his ice-axe into the slope, and more by luck than judgment slithered to a halt less than ten yards from the crevasse. He was shaken, in more ways than one, and from now on his progress was slower and less spectacular.

Nevertheless he made amazingly good time and a little before noon passed the site of Camp I. He had eaten for breakfast only a bowl of half-warmed oatmeal and a thick slice of bread; but he was in too desperate a hurry to stop for another meal; and he stayed a bare ten minutes at Camp I before pushing on for Rongbuk. His descent of Everest took on the nature of a panic-stricken flight. He was determined to spend that night not alone and foodless in his tent, but in the comfort and warmth of Rongbuk, where he could find the sustenance and company he had too long craved for.

Limping and aching, with sweat pouring from his face, he fled like one demented from the mountain he had challenged with such rash and ill-judged assurance.

Soon he passed the junction of the two Rongbuk glaciers, and already it was growing dark. He still had another fifteen hundred feet to descend, along a river valley with steep slopes, precipitous cliffs and difficult loose screes. There was no track. His throat was parched, and the lids of his eyes almost gummed together. His right ankle and left arm were throbbing with dull shafts of pain. But still, refusing to pitch camp he staggered wearily on. Soon the pale uncaring crescent of the moon rose and hung motionless over Everest's North Peak, lighting up his pitiable flight.

Wilson could at times hardly see where he was going. On at least five occasions he fell heavily: and went tumbling down the screes, slipping as much as thirty feet before he caught hold of some rock, or projection that could brake his fall.

His diary gives a prosaic, rather matter-of-fact account of the night's journey; only by reading between the lines is it possible to picture what a macabre nightmare it must have been. "Walked for four hours," he wrote, "by light of new moon. Turned out to be a good pathfinder. If I stumbled, often had to simply let myself go, and went rolling over and over until I hit something. Found myself several times at bottom of deep river valley and had to scramble back up 60-foot slope. Lucky I've got a bump of locality! At last, about 10 p.m., found myself coming up to monastery. Called out to Tewang, and he came rushing up with snow-white teeth and outstretched hand. How delighted the boys were to see me. . . ."

Somehow Wilson had reached safety. He was dazed, half-crippled and half-blinded; but he was alive.

It would have been a creditable feat for a fit and experienced mountaineer to have descended five thousand feet down Everest in a single day; for a man in Wilson's condition—with swollen eyes, constricted throat, wrenched ankle and half-paralysed left arm—it was an almost incredible achievement: an ordeal which would have sapped the strength of any normal man.

Yet that very evening, as he lay exhausted in his tent, he began, while Rinzing and Tewang heated a bowl of soup, to enter up his diary. "Next time," he wrote, in a barely legible scrawl, "I'll take more supplies with me. I'll not give up. I still *know* that I can do it. . . ."

CHAPTER NINE

THE SECOND ASSAULT

H E HAD found the Sherpas camped just outside the monastery. Quickly they came to his aid, and half-supported, half-carried him into a nearby building—a solid stone-built room abutting the main monastery wall. There they partially undressed him and laid him down under a mountain of sheepskins, close to a warming fire.

Soon Rinzing had some hot food ready; first a vegetable soup, then a steaming bowl of fried meat and rice, followed by a mug of tea, with neither sugar nor milk, which Wilson thought "the most wonderful I'd ever had in all my life". Gradually he began to thaw back to normal. His feet seemed at first to be frozen solid; but after about an hour he found he could move his toes and it was obvious that somehow he had managed to escape frostbite. But his throat was still painful, his eyes were swollen and bloodshot, and his arm and ankle throbbed painfully.

As he ate—his first nourishing meal for ten days—he felt strength gradually flowing back into his body; and he felt, too, an unusual but deep-rooted desire for companionship and friendship, and he found himself incoherently telling the Sherpas of all the loneliness, hardship and frustration he had endured on the Rongbuk glacier.

They, in their turn, told him of their anxieties and fears; and Tewang said that only a few hours ago he had seen the Head Lama, and had told him that the next day he was himself going up the glacier to find trace of his leader.

At last Wilson, in the middle of a conversation, fell suddenly asleep. The porters took it in turns to watch over him, and as hour followed hour without his waking they soon began to show no little anxiety. But at last, after thirty-eight hours, Wilson awoke. He found he was too weak even to roll out of his sleeping bag.

A man with more judgment and less courage would, at this stage, have admitted defeat. But the magnitude of his self-appointed task served only to spur Wilson on. The ascent of Everest would, he now realized, be a truly super-human task: a task the fulfilment of which would be certain proof of his own Divine Inspiration. "Weren't we told," he wrote, "that faith could move mountains? If I have faith enough I *know* that I can climb Mount Everest."

Yet though he still seemed to think that God would guide him up the mountain, he planned his second assault with all the care and thoroughness his meagre circumstances would allow. As he lay in the monastery, weak and lethargic, his bloodshot eyes still throbbing with pain, he talked to Rinzing and Tewang and together they laid plans for their next attempt. Tsering had earlier been taken sick with a stomach complaint and was still too ill to accompany them.

It was agreed that the Sherpas would climb with him as far as Camp III, just below the ice-fall guarding the North Col. They would carry between them enough supplies to establish a well-stocked camp, and here they would lie up until the weather seemed set fair and Wilson, alone, could make "a last dive for the summit". In spite of his original contention that large expeditions were unnecessary, Wilson now found himself adopting their well-proved technique. Having found by bitter experience that "the experts" were right in one respect, a wiser man would surely have given up. It was the tragedy of Maurice Wilson's life that he had too much courage and too little wisdom.

But for several weeks his plans for a second assault hung fire; for his recovery took longer than he expected.

He stayed in bed for four days, sleeping and eating by turns; then on the fifth he got up for a couple of hours in the late afternoon. He felt terribly shaky and lethargic, and was glad to get back into his sleeping bag. His feet were still swollen, and his left arm and left eye both throbbed painfully. But towards the end of April his recovery became more rapid. He enjoyed his first bath for weeks in a building next to the monastery cookhouse; and on April 30th wrote: "Feet and eyes very much better, another few days should see me on the job again. Have lost weight tremendously, but have developed many new muscles since leaving Darjeeling. Soon be fit as ever. The trek to Camp III should be comparatively light this time. Shall take crampons, and will have the boys with me to make something hot. Hope to be off in a few more days." But his progress back to fitness was soon to receive a serious set-back. He woke on May 1st to find his left eye badly swollen and the left side of his face partially paralysed. He thought apparently that Tibetan food might somehow be responsible. He had during the last few days deserted his vegetarian diet, and had eaten a good deal of Tibetan meat—a somewhat risky dish for the most hardened of digestions. He decided to fast, which he did for a couple of days; then he returned to a light diet of meal, chupatties and biscuits. Almost at once he felt substantially better.

Soon he moved back into his tent, and began again those long walks which had played so large a part in his original training programme. He took pride in the fact that after a week he could "average fifteen miles a day and not feel the least bit tired". It did not seem to occur to him that he could have spent his time far more profitably in learning to use his ice-axe and crampons.

By May 10th Wilson was ready to begin his second attempt on Everest, but it was now his Sherpas who were far from fit.

Tsering had never become properly acclimatized. Their trek across the Tibetan plateau had been carried out at too fast a pace for him, and even at Rongbuk he still felt lethargic and slightly sick. Obviously he was quite unfit for work on even the lower slopes of Everest. So early in May he and the expedition's single pony left for a small hamlet lower down the valley.

Tewang, since Wilson's return, had been the live-wire of

the party; but on May 6th he developed a stomach ailment. "Doesn't look," wrote Wilson, "as if Tewang will be ready to go for several days." He mixed him up a strange concoction of whisky and flour, thinking he might have dysentery; and the next day he even gave him a stomach massage. But it was the best part of a week before Tewang felt fit enough to accompany Wilson—and even then, as events later proved, he was to be something of a liability.

Rinzing was indeed the only one of the party in apparently perfect health; and it was he who in the weeks ahead shouldered, cheerfully and competently, most of the expedition's burdens.

While he was waiting for Tewang to recover, Wilson made a few last preparations for his final attempt—it would, he knew, be his last chance to tackle Everest that year, for in a few weeks the monsoon was sure to break.

He also began to take a deep interest in the religious life of the Rongbuk Monastery.

It was a way of life that at once surprised and attracted him, and he spent a good deal of time talking, in his somewhat peculiar brand of Tibetan, to the monks.

Life in the monastery, he found was "a mixture of piety, gentleness, laughter and dirt". There was little of the solemn austerity he had half-expected. He found that the life of contemplation to which the monks were dedicated was, above all else, a happy life; even their divine services were bright, cheerful ceremonies, with much singing and drum-beating and gay colourful costumes. But beyond the monastery—which is said to date back over two thousand years and consists of a collection of low, flat-roofed buildings dominated by an immense chorten (a cupola-like monument built in terraces and crowned by emblems of the sun and moon)—there live, far up the Rongbuk Valley, monks of a very different kind. Here in Chamalung, "the Sanctuary of the Birds", dotted among the steep-sided shelves of moraine, are a small nunnery and a collection of primitive cells, where hermits pass a life of meditation, in circumstances of hardship that quite stagger the imagination. Perhaps the most vivid account of their life is Captain John Noel's. "In the heart of this sacred valley," he wrote, "these hermits live, gaining merit so that when they die their souls may escape from the affrighting cycle of reincarnation which they believe to be the inevitable and eternal sequel to the lives of ordinary men. . . . There is one saint, who has been sealed up in a rock cell beneath Mount Everest, dwelling in darkness for fifteen years, meditating, sitting motionless year after year. Once a day brother monks bring a cup of water and a handful of barley meal to this self-isolated priest. I myself watched, and saw through a hole in the wall of the hermit's cell a hand steal out and take in the water and the bread. Even the hand was muffled because not only must no one see him, not even the light of day may touch his skin." Wilson passed many of these remote incredibly isolated cells during his daily twenty-mile hikes; several times he tried to talk to the hermits, but all they told him was that he must be careful to kill no animals or birds in the sanctuary of Chamalung and that they would pray for his success.

At last Tewang's health improved sufficiently for Wilson to fix a definite date for the start of his second attempt—Saturday, May 12th.

He paid far more attention this time to the question of supplies. He bought vast quantities of dates, and baked himself a sack of special biscuits, consisting mainly of brownbread, flour and oats; these he optimistically decided to keep for use "above Camp V, as they are so much lighter and handier than bread". He also stole—there is no other word for it—a seven-pound tin of bull's-eyes from the expedition's stores. There is something rather touching in Wilson's disproportionate joy in this simple find—"they reminded me," he wrote, "of home, of my childhood and of my mother—the only true love I've ever known in life. . . ."

He divided their equipment into three packs—forty-five pounds for Rinzing, thirty-five pounds for himself, and twenty-five pounds for Tewang who was still far from one

The North Col

Camp III . . . .
Eight thousand feet from the summit. (Photograph from the 1936 Expedition)

hundred per cent fit. He also took more climbing equipment, ropes, ice-axes, etc., as well as sun goggles and white cream to alleviate glacial sunburn.

One of his last actions was to give Tewang a deed of assignment for the pony, making him promise that he would not sell it, but would use it for his ride to Lhasa. He also gave him a letter which was, in the event of his death, to be handed on to the authorities in Darjeeling. This letter asked that the three Sherpas should be exonerated from all blame in accompanying him on his forbidden journey.

That evening—May 11th—walking back to his camp, he saw Everest shrouded in mist and looking "very wild". But Wilson was tired of delay, and wrote "in any event we're off tomorrow, come what may. Shall be glad to get the job over."

*　　*　　*

And so in May, 1934, the last inevitable acts of the drama were played out on the northern face of Everest.

As soon as it was light on Saturday, May 12th, Wilson, Tewang and Rinzing left the monastery and set off purpose-fully towards the head of the Rongbuk Valley. Ahead, framed by the early morning mist, Everest's sheer cliffs of ice-draped rock seemed to rise out of the sky itself; but soon the sun broke through, the mists cleared and the mountain was clearly revealed in all her majesty.

It was a lonely, desolate world they were entering; a world

> "Black, wintry, dead, unmeasured, without herb
> Insect, or beast, or shape or sound of life . . ."

and it was bitterly cold. The sun seemed to have lost all warmth. Nevertheless Wilson covered his face with anti-frost and anti-violet-ray cream, and for seven hours the three men climbed steadily up the lower slopes. Soon they passed Ruttledge's base camp and began to work their way along the moraine ledges of the main Rongbuk Glacier. Wilson was

determined to waste no time, and urged the Sherpas forward.
"We must," he said, "reach Camp I tonight."

Tewang, still weakened by his illness, struggled gamely on.
He never uttered a word of complaint, but Wilson could see
that the journey was already sapping his strength.

Wilson himself, was going remarkably well. His earlier
attempt had obviously helped his acclimatization, and the
ascent of 2,300 feet in a day caused him no trouble at all.
Rinzing seemed equally fit.

It was soon after three o'clock that they reached the site of
Camp I, and pitched their tents under a moraine ledge at
the approaches to the East Rongbuk Glacier. Within half
an hour the sun had dipped behind the long arete of the
North Peak and it grew bitterly cold. As Rinzing prepared
the evening meal, Wilson and Tewang sat huddled together
for warmth in the Sherpa's tent. Hot tea soon restored their
spirits; but later that night the cold seemed to penetrate
more keenly than ever before into their tents. Wilson had to
wear mittens while he brought his diary up to date: "My
pencil is like ice," he wrote. At ten o'clock he got out of his
sleeping bag and looked at the thermometer; already it was
recording over eighty degrees of frost. He felt reasonably
warm but sleep that night eluded him. He blamed the tea:
"Damned tea was like soup and is keeping me awake. Must
show Tewang how to brew it. We are using China tea, com-
pressed in the shape of a brick and a little goes a long way.
They will overdo it." Nevertheless in the early hours of
March 13th he dozed off, and awoke at dawn reasonably
fresh. Tewang had slept badly.

The next day they again made good progress. Rinzing
appreciated that on his first attempt Wilson had failed to eat
sufficient hot, nourishing food—at altitudes of over twenty
thousand feet it is quite impossible for a man to exist for
long on his bodily heat alone—and this time he insisted on
preparing a hot breakfast. While this was being cooked and
the two Sherpas took turns at working the bellows, Wilson
did a little reconnaissance and hit on a good lead. They

started off at 8 a.m., and were soon climbing at a speed which put Wilson's previous efforts in the shade. The Sherpas proved invaluable in picking exactly the right route and in helping Wilson along the few difficult ledges. This day too they climbed a little over 2,000 feet, reaching Camp II at 3 p.m. and settling there for the night. "Gorgeous day," wrote Wilson. "Weather perfect—cold but sunny and no sign of the monsoon. Here we are at Camp II after what seemed like a spring walk compared to my last effort."

An hour's blowing with the bellows brought their tea water to the boil, and Wilson measured out sufficient tea for his own liking, doubtless the Sherpas later trebled this for their own tea, but Wilson at least got a brew to his satisfaction. The three men were in good spirits. Tewang felt if anything a little stronger—Wilson was full of confidence. And Rinzing was so inexhaustible that he spent several hours looking for Wilson's rucksack, which the latter had dropped here during the descent; the rucksack had a jersey in it, and this Wilson had promised to Rinzing. At about eight o'clock, in pitch darkness, the Sherpa finally stumbled across it at the edge of a small drift. He took it in triumph to Wilson's tent and appeared next morning wearing the promised jersey. Unfortunately, they could not find the crampons, thrown aside by Wilson on his first assault.

Monday, May 14th, was another fine day: and a day too of excellent progress.

They had breakfasted and struck camp by eight o'clock, and the Sherpas showed Wilson the easiest route—the one used by Ruttledge—into the great glacier troughs. Well before noon they were pushing strongly upward among the great seracs and pinnacles that rose, up to one hundred feet in height, all around them. As morning passed into afternoon they began to suffer from the inevitable glacier lassitude, Tewang especially had to make frequent halts to regain his breath; but towards the head of the trough the gradient eased off and the going became if anything a little easier.

Wilson had given his cork-insulated boots to Rinzing, and was wearing the Sherpa's felt-lined ones; he found that in these he could keep his footing more easily. Nevertheless he several times fell heavily on the polished surface of the ice—he badly missed the crampons which would have given him a sure foothold. Over the few difficult places he cut inexpert but effective steps with his ice-axe, it amazed him how much effort it required to dislodge even a few splinters of the tough, rubbery ice.

Soon after noon they passed the site of Wilson's highest camp on his first assault, and an hour later the trough began to peter out among the upper reaches of the East Rongbuk Glacier. Here the wind and the flying snow came tearing down on them—in sudden contrast to the almost-warm and stagnant air of the trough. They were at 21,000 feet. Only a little way ahead lay the desolate and windswept site of Ruttledge's Camp III.

Bowed low against the wind the three men struggled forward into one of the most breath-taking vistas in the world.

Quite suddenly the long northern buttress of Changtse (the North Peak) fell away behind them, and the upper slopes of Everest herself, hitherto hidden, rose suddenly and steeply before them; six thousand feet of snow-encrusted slab and avalanche-swept couloir, and beyond, the white, rock-strewn cone of the summit trailing its plume of windswept snow far into Nepal. At last the upper slopes of Everest were tangible, clearly revealed, no longer the fabric of dreams and visions. There, for Wilson to see, was the way to the summit, and in the bright, clear atmosphere it looked comparatively near. Wilson at that moment must surely have had visions of success.

But his dreams of the future were quickly shattered by the reality of the present. Their immediate concern was to pitch camp and give the exhausted Tewang some sort of shelter, for the Sherpa was clearly in much distress; his breathing was fast and irregular, and he was doubled up with stomach cramp. They helped him towards the site of

Camp III, half-way between the head of the glacier and the beginning of the great ice-fall which rose 1,500 feet above them to the shoulder of the North Col. It was surely one of the most bleak and desolate places in the world, the sport of tearing winds, and veils of snow ripped from the ice-fall and driven horizontally across the glacier-head; but it was the only level site that was reasonably free from the danger of avalanches which daily cascaded their millions of tons of ice down the approaches to North Col. Here among the moraine boulders and snow drifts, at about three o'clock, they set up their two tents, and into one Tewang collapsed utterly exhausted. Rinzing set about preparing their meal, and Wilson, after making sure that Tewang was as warm and comfortable as possible, walked a little way toward the foot of the ice fall.

The sun was dipping below the ridge of the north-west arete as he saw, rising steeply above him and only some few hundred yards away, the broken ramparts of the ice-fall that were his first really difficult mountaineering problem. He must have understood then how pitiably ill-equipped he was to fulfill his quest.

The approaches to the North Col consist of a steep broken ice fall which rises some 1,500 feet from the upper reaches of the East Rongbuk Glacier to the crest of the col itself. As the ice fall is continually being pushed forward and downward its slopes present a different appearance from year to year. The two expeditions of the 1920's and the Ruttledge expedition all found it a difficult obstacle to surmount—and these expeditions included some of the finest ice-climbers of the first half of the century. Yet Wilson, who could hardly cut an efficient step, was apparently quite undaunted.

But it was nevertheless a grim, forbidding scene that opened out in front of him.

To his left lay a series of precipitous ice-cliffs, each some hundred to two hundred feet in height, rising one above the other, with narrow shelves between. The face of most of them was sheer, clean-cut and quite unclimbable, while some had great overhanging bulges which threatened at any moment to avalanche into the East Rongbuk Glacier. Ahead, in the direction of the route followed in 1924, lay a clean-swept slope of ice rising steeply to the base of a 400-foot precipitous cliff; the slope itself was perfectly climbable, but at its foot lay the tumbled debris of many an avalanche, and the cliff at its head made it an obvious cul-de-sac. Only to the right—in the general direction of the 1922 route—did the ice fall appear to be even remotely climbable. Here, the lower slopes were steep—steep enough to necessitate almost continual step-cutting; but they were kept free from avalanches by a great crevasse half-way up the fall which split it horizontally, and was wide enough to engulf all avalanches coming down from the upper slopes. The crevasse, however did not appear to be bridged; and whether it could in fact be crossed was something only a detailed on-the-spot inspection would disclose. Beyond the crevasse the slopes eased off a little, but the last fifty to a hundred feet seemed to consist of a sheer ice cliff, almost vertical, which would have to be taken by frontal assault. There seemed, however, at one point to be a chimney reaching almost to the top. Above this last ice cliff lay the North Col where Camp IV, at some 23,000 feet, would have to be established.

As Wilson wrote that night in his diary, "Summit and route to it can be seen quite clearly now. Only another 8,000 feet to go." But what a formidable 8,000 feet they were!

*   *   *

It was almost dark by the time he returned to Camp III. Rinzing had managed to make some rather lukewarm tea, and once they had finished this he suggested to Wilson that they make their way to Ruttledge's store-dump, which he felt certain was only a few hundred yards distant. There, he said, they would find any number of delicacies to add to their own somewhat inadequate supplies—in all probability he was heartily sick by now of Wilson's dates and oatmeal! It says much for the fitness of the two men that at eight o'clock that night they ventured out on the windswept glacier to search for Ruttledge's supply-dump. After about ten minutes they lost each other in the pitch darkness, and Wilson returned to his tent. He was still thawing out his feet, half an hour later, when there was a heaving and grunting outside and after a moment Rinzing came staggering in.

He had carried a forty-pound provision box for several hundred yards through the wind and darkness that engulfed the glacier. And he stood, licking his lips, while Wilson forced open the wooden crate. Out came a veritable stream of delicacies—honey, butter, cheese, anchovy paste, cream and chocolate biscuits and tins of soup and meat. Wilson was delighted. The Sherpas had told him of the cache, but he had hardly expected such a treasure as this. "We'll talk tomorrow about a Santa Claus party outside my tent," he wrote.

It was, however, too late and too cold to think of cooking that night. So they contented themselves with chocolate biscuits and Wilson promised them an orgy the following day. And the three men settled down to sleep.

The next day, May 15th, was again fine. But Wilson, who had slept poorly, decided to lie up for the day before attempting the ice fall. In his excitement the night before, he had forgotten to level off the floor of his tent and he had spent most of the night rolling down on to an unpleasantly sharp boulder that lay alongside the tent wall.

After a day of rest, during which Wilson discarded any thought of dieting and sampled most of the previous expedition's stores, the three men felt ready to tackle the ice fall early the next morning. Rinzing was especially energetic; and, delighted at the pleasure the food-boxes gave Wilson, he fetched another. Wilson's diary, which he wrote up early that night, mentions nothing but food: "Eaten almost everything in sight today. Soup, Ovaltine and heaven knows what. Rinzing went for another box and this had great variety of stores including maple-sugar, cake and

vegetable extract. You couldn't guess what I'm wallowing
in as I write! A 1 lb. box of King George chocs!" Hopes
were high that night—higher perhaps than they were ever
to be again; for the next day Wilson's diary was briefly
expressive:

"*May 16th. Wed.* Weather rotten. Still at Camp III."

And five days later they were still pinned down to their
exposed and windswept site by the blizzards which raged
continuously about the northern face of Everest.

It seems that the weather in 1934 was especially bad on
Everest. Usually there are six or seven weeks, from mid-
April to the end of May, when the mountain is—at least in
theory—climbable. Up to April winter conditions prevail
and the upper slopes are quite unapproachable because of
wind, storm and cold. After the end of May the warm wet
winds of the monsoon, blowing up from the south turn the
Himalayan peaks into a death trap of crumbling ice walls
and thundering avalanches. Only in the late spring do
conditions offer the slightest chance of success, and even in
these few weeks the mountain is guarded by cold, wind,
avalanche and blizzard, worse only in degree to those of
winter. There are seldom more than two or three days together when climbing is practicable; and each year the
weather conditions differ slightly and present their own
particular problems. It seems that 1934 was a year of ex-
tremes, with one or two perfect days followed by prolonged
blizzards of unusual fury.

Such a blizzard now enveloped Camp III.

Day after day the three men remained huddled together
in their tents, which the wind threatened hourly to pluck
up and hurl down the East Rongbuk Glacier. At least they
had plenty of food, but the dull continuous roar of the wind
and the numbing cold must have gradually sapped their
strength.

At first Wilson's entries in his diary were long and optimistic—if sadly out of touch with reality; but gradually
they became shorter and tinged with something like despair.

"*May* 17*th. Thurs.* It's snowing like the devil, and I can see less than 200 feet. Had bit of a head, but shall start tomorrow if weather O.K. Have decided not to take short cut to Camp V as at first intended as should have to cut my own steps up the ice-fall; that's silly when there should already be handrope and steps leading to old Camp IV." (It seems that Wilson seriously expected the steps cut by Ruttledge over a year ago to be still intact.) "Not much to do except eat and sleep. What do you think I had yesterday? Anchovy paste from Fortnum and Masons! Usually we feed twice a day. First about 6.30 when Rintsi comes along with smoked tea or Ovaltine, followed half an hour later by soup with meat in it. Then at 2 p.m. up comes the same again. Everything tastes horribly of smoke. . . !"

"*May* 18*th. Fri.* Nothing to do all day. . . . It's still snowing and blowing like the D. Went to see how the boys were getting on at 3 p.m., but was soon glad to get back to sleeping bag. Rintsi went to store dump and got some fine Ever-Ready batteries—a darned sight better than those we bought in Darjeeling. He also bagged a 20 ft. bamboo mast for firewood; doesn't go to the bother of breaking it up, but has the thing propped its whole length across fire and pulls in the slack as it burns away. . . . Just going to have a bit of shut eye."

"*May* 19*th. Sat.* Another couple of days and it will be 12 months since I said cheerio to you all. How time flies. Weather still too windy and far too much drift snow to start off today, so am just sitting or rather lying quiet. Feeling bit better after long lay up out of sun."

"*May* 20*th. Sun.* Snow stopped and sun out but wind still v. bad. These violet rays are terrible. Have thick blanket strapped over tent, but can still feel them through my balaclava helmet. When I've had my Irish Stew shall have to get out yet another helmet."

"*May* 21*st. Mon.* Had enough bed the last few days for a year. Terrible when you can't put your head down for aching nerves. Weather better. We start again tomorrow."

And the next day, almost a year after he had left England, Wilson started on the penultimate stage of his lone assault. He had slept badly on the night of the 21st and woke feeling cold; he found himself shivering as he waited for Rinzing to brew up the tea, and took twenty minutes to lace up his climbing boots. He breakfasted as the pale light of dawn came flooding coldly over the rim of North Col. Then he looked outside the tent and saw the crest of Everest, snow-plumed and deceptively near. The wind had dropped, and as the sun came streaming over the eastern peaks he began to climb, very slowly, towards the ice fall.

Rinzing had promised to come with him until it was noon to show him the approximate route used by Ruttledge; and to start with the two men made reasonable progress up the lower slopes. But soon the gradient steepened, the ice became broken into monstrous blocks and seracs, and the newly-fallen snow masked the host of minor crevasses that split the face of the ice in all directions. Wilson looked about in vain for traces of the track hewn out by Ruttledge; the steps had been destroyed and the rope guides swept away. An hour after breaking camp they began to cut steps.

Wilson was so inexpert at this that he had to ask Rinzing to lead, and he watched the Sherpa carefully to see how the steps were made. After twenty minutes he took over the lead, but soon found that the additional effort of step cutting quickly sapped his energy—probably his lack of skill meant that his exertions were far greater than those of an experienced mountaineer. Soon they came to an especially steep slope, of some sixty degrees, crowned by a number of unstable-looking seracs. Their progress was reduced to a panting crawl.

It took them a couple of hours to cut steps up the forty feet of slope; but at last they emerged on to a narrow ledge among the grotesque seracs and pinnacles. At one end of the ledge a steep little couloir led upwards towards the great crevasse.

It was after noon and Rinzing told Wilson he could come

no further, as darkness would fall before he could make the descent to Camp III. They shook hands and the Sherpa began to retrace his steps. Soon he had vanished from sight, and Wilson felt very much alone.

He worked his way among the seracs to the foot of the little couloir; it looked, from close to, even steeper than he had feared. It was two o'clock now, and realizing he could hardly climb it that night, Wilson decided to pitch camp. It was difficult to find a spot level enough to set up his tent, and he was tempted to make use of the open space at the foot of the couloir. There, however, the ground had been worn smooth by the passage of countless small avalanches, which periodically came sweeping down the couloir and then, after some fifty feet, cascaded over the steepening cliff. He decided—wisely—to prefer the discomfort of the seracs to the danger of the avalanches, and eventually managed to wedge his tent, at a somewhat alarming angle, between two reasonably stable pinnacles.

He was exhausted; and now he was alone he began once again to neglect his health. He could not be bothered to prepare a proper meal, but ate only some chocolate and dry biscuits before crawling into his sleeping-bag. He wanted desperately to sleep, but sleep did not come easily. Surely that night he must have been haunted by the spectre of impending failure; he had planned to reach the col by nightfall, but he was only some third of the way there. And tomorrow he would be alone.

May 23rd dawned mercifully fine. He was up early and cooked himself a good breakfast of hot stew; but he was surprised to find how long everything took. He had woken at six; it was seven-thirty before he had cooked breakfast, and after nine before he had struck camp. The sun's rays were surprisingly warm on his back as a little before ten o'clock he stood looking up at the couloir. Wilson hoped that the milder weather did not herald the approach of the monsoon. From higher up on the shoulder of Everest he could hear the distant roar of avalanches, and he dreaded being caught by one in the couloir. He knew it was near here that in 1922 seven porters had been killed by avalanching snow. He began, slowly, laboriously and inexpertly cutting steps up the edge of the couloir, avoiding the centre which he saw was liable to avalanche. And as morning passed into afternoon he must have realized the hopelessness of his task.

For his headway was pitiably slow and cost him great effort. Every few minutes he had to stop and gasp for breath. Once his foothold gave way, and he slid back for twenty feet, starting a small avalanche, which, as he watched it, gained in bulk and momentum and went cascading down the ice fall until, far below, it shot down and outward on to the East Rongbuk Glacier.

It took him three hours to climb the couloir. Then, still cutting steps, he traversed the slope that led up sharply toward the great crevasse. He pitched camp in a poor position on a shelf, tilted at twenty degrees, in the middle of the windswept slope. A blizzard would have blown him straight on to the glacier, now nearly a thousand feet below. But he was lucky. The night was calm, though terribly cold. At 4 p.m. too exhausted to prepare a meal, he fell into his sleeping-bag. "Just," he wrote, "going to have a few minutes shut-eye." When he woke it was dawn and he was bitterly cold.

There had in the night been fifty-seven degrees of frost and Wilson feared he must surely have frost-bite. But after a couple of hours he found he could move both fingers and toes, and it was clear that he had somehow escaped it. He had, however, a headache, and a throat which two cups of luke-warm tea did little to alleviate. He ate a small quantity of snow, and then at 9 a.m. started off again.

His first obstacle was the crevasse.

He approached it cautiously, which was just as well, for it proved to have an unstable lower lip and looked quite bottomless. It averaged some thirty feet in width, and its walls were sheer, pale blue at the top, merging into royal blue, deep blue and indigo as it plummeted into unseen depths. Wilson worked his way along it, keeping to the left where the crevasse seemed to narrow slightly. After about an hour he came to an unstable-looking snow bridge.

Snow bridges present a tricky problem even to the experienced mountaineer; there is no certain way of gauging their strength. Wilson tried for a couple of hours to find an alternative route over the crevasse. There was none. He sat down and ate his lunch—five dry biscuits. Then, because postponement of the issue was obviously no solution to it, he knelt down and prayed and when he had finished he got up and walked across the bridge as carefully as he could. And the bridge held.

When he reached the other side he found a not too difficult slope, which he traversed with the cutting of only a few steps for some hundred and fifty yards. Then, at about noon, he reached the foot of the last ice cliff, guarding the comparatively easy slopes to the North Col. Another two hundred feet and he would reach the col. He looked in vain for some crack in the apparently unscalable face: sixty feet of ice and rock, not only vertical but actually in some places overhanging. He remembered the chimney he had seen from Camp III, but in his pre-occupation with crossing the crevasse, he realized he had worked away from it. He started to hack his way along the foot of the cliff apparently oblivious to the danger of avalanches, and at last, more by luck than judgment, found himself working toward the chimney.

That night when he pitched camp at its foot, he was at a height of only a little under 23,000 feet. Once again he was too exhausted to cook a meal. Nor did he choose a good site for his tent—it would in all probability have been impossible to find a "good" site on the ice fall, but Wilson was too weary to find even a passable one. He set up his tent at an angle of thirty-five degrees and scooped and hacked away the snow and ice to prevent his rolling down the icefall in his sleep.

He spent a miserable night.

The dawn of May 24th saw him crawl very slowly out of

his tent and prepare his breakfast, "took 2 hours for damned water to boil". He used his matches as an improvised candle-stand, and they soon became useless—saturated with grease. Wilson realized he now had no means of making either heat or light. But he refused to give up.

For seven hours he tried to climb the chimney.

How far up he got we shall never know—probably not very far. But the fact that he failed to climb it is not really important; what matters is that he went on trying. The odds are that an experienced mountaineer could probably have climbed the chimney in about an hour—though even this is by no means certain as it may not have been on the exact route used by Ruttledge, or if it was, its composition may have altered. In any case it was, for Wilson, an insurmount-able obstacle: every difficulty he had so far met with he had overcome. But here was a barrier that courage and deter-mination alone could never break. By the end of May 24th, when he stumbled into his tent, still at the foot of the chim-ney, he must have known with terrible certainty that he would never climb Mount Everest alone.

The next day, having neither drunk nor eaten anything hot for over twenty-four hours, he set out again. But he was too weak to climb more than a few yards above his tent.

He realized that he was now faced with the same three courses as on the East Rongbuk Glacier a month before. He could climb up the chimney until he fell to his death; he could stay in his tent and wait for death to come to him; or he could go back, and try to persuade the Sherpas to accom-pany him still higher.

Wilson had still sufficient sanity to realize that only the last course afforded him the slightest hope of reaching the top of Everest. It seems from his diary—which from now on becomes slightly incoherent and extremely difficult to read —that he hoped to return to Camp III, rest there for a couple of days and then persuade Rinzing to carry supplies for him up to Camp IV; he evidently had sufficient faith in the Sherpa's mountaineering skill to believe that the two of them could between them climb the chimney on to the slopes of North Col.

And so at about ten o'clock Wilson began his second flight from Everest; a flight even more incredible than the first.

In less than five hours, weak and unskilled as he was, he slipped and slithered his way down fifteen hundred feet of extremely difficult ice. Twice he fell badly, and rolled over and over until the soft snow checked him. Each time he struggled quickly to his feet, rubbing the pain from his ribs; they might for all he knew have been broken; he had no time to find out; he only knew that somehow he must reach Camp III before nightfall. He came to the crevasse, and the snow bridge looked even frailer than before; but once again it held. He found his steps down the couloir, and half scrambled, half fell down them. In the twilight haze he could pick out far below him, the tents of Camp III. He saw the Sherpas stumbling upward to meet him, and almost sobbing with relief he fell into Rinzing's arms and was carried into his tent. A bowl of hot soup and then, quite literally half-dead with exhaustion, he fell asleep. And he slept for thirty hours.

He woke at 11 p.m. on Saturday, May 26th, and his Sherpas had a hot meal ready and waiting. Their kindness and their obvious anxiety touched Wilson deeply; but when they spoke of returning to Rongbuk he simply shook his head.

"I didn't come back," he said, "because I'd given up—I came back because I want you to come with me to Camp IV."

CHAPTER TEN

"IF I DON'T COME BACK . . ."

Up to now Wilson's battered little diary has provided a fairly complete account of his day-by-day progress on to the upper slopes of Everest. But for the last days of his life the diary entries are short and pitiably incoherent; thus of his third attempt to climb the mountain we can gain only a blurred fragmentary picture.

We know that on Saturday and Sunday he remained resting in his tent. His diary simply reads:

"26th *Sat.* Stayed in bed.

27th *Sun.*   ,,   ,,

and we can imagine him, most of the time asleep, curled up in his bag, while the Sherpas in their tent a few yards away cooked food and probably reflected on the hopelessness of their position; and the wind tore and thundered around them incessantly, and the cold and the inhuman desolation sapped away the very desire to live.

It must by now have been obvious to Wilson that if he went on alone, it could only be to his death; and he must therefore have used all his eloquence to try to persuade the Sherpas to accompany him at least to the top of the ice fall. And by the night of Sunday 27th, he apparently believed that his eloquence had taken effect; for he wrote next morning in his diary: "28th *Mon.* Tewang wanted to go back, but persuaded them go with me to Camp V. This will be last effort, and I feel successful. . . ."

But in actual fact either he had misunderstood the Sherpas or else his mind had begun to wander—it is quite common for those who stay too long at high altitudes to suffer from delusions—for Tewang and Rinzing soon made it abundantly plain that under no circumstances would they go a step further.

"Off again. Gorgeous day" . . . the last entries
in Wilson's diary

Mount Everest . . . it conquered the man

Tewang indeed was in no shape to continue, it would be as much as he could manage safely to descend, let alone ascend, the mountain; and Rinzing, who had climbed to over 27,000 feet on the previous expedition, knew enough about the upper slopes of Everest to realize that even if they climbed the ice fall the summit would still be utterly beyond them. Both the Sherpas, men born and bred in the high hills of the Himalaya, men whose judgment was far more balanced than that of Wilson, said emphatically that it was impossible to push on further. It was too late, they said; in a few days the monsoon would break; they pointed out that they were all too weak (Wilson was partially snow-blinded and suffering from exhaustion and lack of oxygen); they had not enough porters, they said, or enough climbing equipment to force a way up the ice fall and establish on the col a well-stocked camp; and, last but by no means least, they knew that Wilson lacked the technical mountaineering skill to lead the ascent safely. With every justification, the Sherpas pleaded with him to abandon his attempt. With every justification, they refused to climb even another fifty feet.

And some time during that afternoon of Monday, May 28th, it must have become plain to Wilson that Tewang and Rinzing would indeed come with him no further.

"Faith," he had once written, "is not faith that wavers when its prayers remain unanswered." Did he still, he must now have asked himself, hold fast to his original belief? Now that it seemed as though God had deserted him, now that all his theories seemed about to be disproved, did he still believe that he could climb Mount Everest alone?

His was the sort of faith that remains inviolate in the face of all adversity, and he began that night to make preparations for his last attempt.

He rummaged about among his kit until he found the "flag of friendship"—the silk pennant on which his closest friends had signed their names before he left London. He decided to take it with him. He also put into his rucksack the oxygen equipment and the bare minimum of supplies;

he knew he would have to travel light, and he took with him food for only seven days; he reckoned if all went well he could climb the mountain in four or five days, and the exhilaration of success would sustain him on his descent.

He had a hot meal that Sunday night at a little before six-thirty; then as he struggled into his sleeping bag, there came over him the strangest feeling; he became convinced that someone was by his side. The only sound was the tearing roar of the wind. The two Sherpas lay resting in their tent. Yet still Wilson felt that he was not alone. "Strange," he wrote, "but I feel that there is somebody with me in tent all the time."

And before this feeling is attributed to an unbalanced state of mind, it should perhaps be remembered that Frank Smythe had undergone a similar experience on the upper slopes of Everest the year before, an experience that he writes about very vividly. "All the time," he tells us, "that I was climbing alone, I had the feeling that there was someone with me. I felt that were I to slip I should be held up and supported as though I had a companion with me with a rope. Sir Ernest Shackleton had the same experience when crossing the mountains of South Georgia after his hazardous open-boat journey from Elephant Island, and he narrates how he and his companion felt that there was an extra 'someone' in the party. When I reached the ledge I felt I ought to eat something to keep up my strength. All I had brought with me was a slab of Kendal Mint Cake. This I took out of my pocket and, carefully dividing it into two halves, turned round with one half in my hand to offer my companion . . ."

That night Wilson slept reasonably well, and the next morning—Tuesday, May 29th—he was up early and as soon as it was light he went across to the Sherpas' tent.

It was chillingly cold and a long banner of snow streamed from the summit of Everest. The wind was very strong, and after covering even the few paces to the porters' tent, Wilson found himself gasping for breath. He came straight to the point. He told them he was determined to make a last attempt. Would they, he asked, come with him? Again Tewang and Rinzing refused; under no circumstances, they said, would they climb another step.

There was, in later years, some talk of the Sherpas having deserted Wilson; but both the word and also its implication of disloyalty are quite out of place. For only if they had made with their leader a joint suicide pact could the Sherpas have been reasonably expected to throw away their lives by joining in so foredoomed a venture.

It was a sad little drama that was, early that morning, played out to its inevitable climax in the porters' tent. The more Tewang and Rinzing pleaded with Wilson to return, the more obstinate he became. When at last he realized he would never get them to change their minds, he must have known in his heart what the end of his quest would be; but he ended the argument by saying simply:

"Wait here for ten days. Then if I don't come back, return by yourselves."

He went out, packed up his tent, his sleeping-bag and his few pieces of equipment. Then, alone and very slowly, he began to climb up the ice fall towards the slopes of the North Col.

He did not get very far.

Just how much he suffered in those last days is something that will never be known; and this perhaps is as it should be, for the Calvary of a brave man is something strictly personal between that man and his God. But the half-dozen lines in his diary and the reports of the Sherpas when they returned later to Kalimpong give the bare facts.

*   *   *

It was in the latter half of July that the first rumours of Wilson's death began to filter through to the outside world. His three Sherpas had returned to Kalimpong; here they were interviewed, interrogated and cross-examined for week after week, and though their story contained a number of inconsistencies, it did, at least, seem to establish the certainty of Wilson's death.

So on July 20th papers all over the world blazoned out their headlines—"Lone Death on Everest", "Pluck or Suicide", "Excelsior with a Union Jack". The publicity would have pleased Wilson, though he would have noticed a little sadly that no mention was ever made of the motive behind his solitary challenge. "What?" is always an easier question to answer than "Why?"

When the evidence of the Sherpas had been correlated, filtered and checked, the gist of it did not amount to much; indeed all they had to say could be, and was, condensed into three short articles printed on July 20th by three London newspapers. Because each of these reports adds a little more to our understanding of the final drama, their relevant passages are quoted in full:

Daily Telegraph

DRAMA OF
LONE EVEREST
CLIMBER

Left his Porters   Diet of Bread and
behind   Porridge

FEAR THAT HE HAS
PERISHED

BEYOND CAMP III ON
THE RUTTLEDGE PATH

It is feared that Mr. Maurice Wilson, the young British airman who was making a gallant attempt to climb Mount Everest alone, has lost his life.

News received here (Darjeeling) today states that his effort to conquer the world's highest peak has ended in tragedy. The porters who accompanied this "Do-or-Die" Briton relate a dramatic story of how, at a height of over 21,000 feet he went on alone, carrying only a light tent, three loaves of bread, two tins of porridge and a camera. . . .

Two porters accompanied him as far as the site of the Camp III —21,000 feet—established by the Ruttledge Expedition. They then deemed it impossible to make farther progress up Mount Everest without ropes and more men to hew the track. But Mr. Wilson, according to the porters there and then decided to go on alone. . . .

After Camp III the track lies over a glacier on which avalanches are constantly crashing down, and there are also treacherous crevasses. The temperature there must have exceeded fifty degrees of frost.

Mountaineers regard this region as one where only experienced, roped parties have a reasonable prospect of getting through.

On the same morning the *Daily Mail* carried the following headlines:

BRITON'S
LONE DEATH
ON EVEREST

CROSSED FRONTIER
IN DISGUISE

FORBIDDEN CLIMB

3 LOAVES AND 2 TINS
OF PORRIDGE

Mr. Maurice Wilson, the 38-year-old Londoner who went out alone at three o'clock on the morning of May 31st in a forbidden attempt to conquer Mount Everest and battle with the treacherous crevasses and avalanches of the Himalaya, is reported by returned porters to have lost his life at a height of 23,000 feet.

From our own Correspondent. Calcutta, Thursday.

On his gallant solo effort to beat the world's highest peak, Mr. Wilson carried with him a light tent, three loaves of bread, two tins of porridge and a camera. The camera was to prove to the world that he had achieved his object.

The details of the drama, of which the last stages were played at a height of 21,000 feet in a temperature of fifty degrees of frost, with the lone European and two native porters as the sole actors, have just become known in Calcutta upon the return of the porters.

Yesterday came news that the gallant effort—which the Maharajah of Nepal had sternly forbidden the previous year when Mr. Wilson wanted to fly over the mountain—had ended in tragedy.

"CERTAIN DEATH"

Mr. Wilson asked the porters to wait a fortnight for him after he had gone on alone.

They declare that they waited three weeks and, as there was still no sign of him, they returned to Kalimpong.

The porters who accompanied Mr. Wilson relate how at a height of 21,000 feet, he went on despite their continued pleading to avoid what they regarded as certain death.

As Mr. Wilson did not return, they surmise that he must have perished in the dangerous region at a height of about 23,000 feet.

The last report appeared that same morning in the paper that had—above all others—always been particularly in sympathy with Wilson's quest: the *Daily Express*.

LONE CLIMBER DEAD
ON EVEREST?

MAN WHO CARRIED A
UNION JACK

LAST SEEN PLODDING OVER THE
ICE WITH HIS PACK

> *Daily Express* Correspondent,
> Calcutta, Thursday.

It is feared that Mr. Maurice Wilson, the Bradford man who set out to plant a Union Jack on the summit of Mount Everest, has perished in the attempt.

The porters who accompanied Mr. Wilson for part of the way have returned to Darjeeling after waiting in vain for the lone climber to return from the top-most slopes of the mountain.

They state that when the party reached a height of 21,000 feet and found the camp established by last year's Everest expedition, they pointed out to Mr. Wilson that it was impossible to proceed further without more porters and ropes. But he decided to go on alone.

When they saw him last he was crossing a glacier carrying a light tent, three loaves of bread, two tins of porridge, a ciné-camera—and his Union Jack.

The report went on to describe how Wilson had travelled to Everest disguised as a Tibetan priest and had covered the distance in a record twenty-five days. "This is regarded as a splendid achievement," added the report, "especially as most of the route was covered at night." It continued:

Mr. Wilson hoped to find the tracks of last year's expedition and lengths of rope abandoned by previous climbers. But in this he was disappointed.

After he left the porters his route lay over a glacier, which is the scene of frequent avalanches. It has treacherous crevasses and the temperature is fifty degrees below freezing point.

Mountaineers regard this region as one where only an experienced party roped together have a reasonable prospect of getting through.

It is surmised that Mr. Wilson met his death in that treacherous area, at an altitude of 23,000 feet.

As a lone feat, his achievement in getting so far with such scanty equipment was a magnificent effort, but there is little hope that he can still be alive.

Apart from these three articles—and a host of others which give either similar or unreliable evidence—our only source of information is the last few entries of Wilson's diary, reproduced opposite page 144. From this scanty material we can piece together the broad outline of the last three days of his life.

* * *

Early on the morning of Tuesday 29th, we can picture Wilson as again he left Camp III and struggled about half-way up the ice-fall. He must have been very weak and the wind that day was high; but he crawled on, inch by painful inch, until he reached a spot some little way above the great crevasse. There, utterly exhausted, he had to give up. It was failure once again. He retraced his steps and camped that night below the crevasse, probably only a little higher than Camp III.

On May 30th he was too weak to leave his sleeping bag and too weak, too, to scrawl more than a single faint line in his diary, "Stayed in bed."

Then on Thursday, May 31st, he set out for the last time. The sun was shining brightly as he packed up his tent and sleeping bag; but its rays, at 21,500 feet held little warmth. Nevertheless it was fine, and Wilson wrote that morning in his diary: "Off again, gorgeous day." These were his last words. He tried to write more, but the message appears only as an incoherent scrawl. Another day of battling with the seracs and crevasses of the ice fall brought an end to his lone assault on Everest. That evening, again utterly exhausted, quite alone, and with the numbing cold of death already seeping into him, he stumbled down to the foot of the fall. There he pitched his tent, only a few hundred feet above Camp III.

Probably he hoped to rest there for another day, before renewing his assault. But the flame of his life was now burning low, and some time that night, or very early the next morning, he died—we can only hope in his sleep—of cold and exhaustion and exposure.

Everest had conquered the man, but not his spirit. That surely was borne up, seven thousand feet, to where the long plume of wind-torn snow began to stream south-eastward across the border of Nepal. And perhaps he was welcomed there by Mallory, and other men, who gave their lives in search of an ideal.

*   *   *

A year was to pass before men again set foot on Everest. Then, early in July, 1935, a party led by Eric Shipton arrived at the foot of the mountain. Their object was reconnaissance rather than a full-scale assault. And with them, for his first

encounter with Everest, came a young Sherpa named
Tenzing. At Rongbuk they were blessed by the Head Lama,
who spoke warmly of the man who had, a year before, dis-
appeared on the upper slopes of the Goddess Mother of the
World. Then the party pushed on up the East Rongbuk
Glacier.

On July 9th Shipton found the body of Maurice Wilson.

He was lying at the very foot of the icefall, only some few
hundred yards above Camp III. His tent had been swept
away by the fury of the monsoon and winter storms; and all
that remained of it were the guy-lines, held down by boulders. Wilson was dressed in his windproof clothing: with his
rucksack by his side.

There was now a sense of tranquillity about the mountain.
The storms had, for the moment, died away. The glacier
and ice-fall were still free of snow, and the scene gave no hint
of the struggle for life that had taken place here eleven months
before.

Shipton held a simple funeral service.

Maurice Wilson's body was buried in a ten-foot snow
crevasse; as Shipton said later, "When we tipped it in, it
completely disappeared. There was no hole where it fell,
just plain white snow." A cairn was raised over the grave,
and Shipton collected Wilson's diary and brought it back to
England.

* * *

So ends the story of Maurice Wilson. At the time of his
death there were few to mourn for him; for he was, to those
who read of his exploits, an object more of pity than of
admiration. It was as though Longfellow had already provided him with an epitaph:

> "There in the twilight cold and grey,
> Lifeless, but beautiful, he lay,
> And from the sky, serene and far,
> A voice fell, like a falling star,
> Excelsior!"

Nor in the years that followed was much attention paid to his lone quixotic challenge. Of the many hundred thousand words written about Everest and the men who tried to climb her, only a few hundred were devoted to Maurice Wilson.

Yet did he really die in vain? Must he be remembered only as a pitiable failure? Should we not rather recall the words of George Leigh-Mallory as he stood at the summit of a great Himalaya peak: "Have we vanquished an enemy?" he asked himself. And the answer was, "None but ourselves. . . . Have we gained success? That word means nothing here." It is true that if we judge him by results, or by his technical skill, Wilson was no great mountaineer. He never in all his life climbed a single worth-while peak. But his spirit was that of Mallory. He failed to conquer Everest; but he never failed himself, or mankind, or his ideal. He possessed, in spite of all his faults—his recklessness and foolish pride—the spirit that makes men great.

No four words could tell more clearly a man's character than those pencilled, very faintly, as the last entry of Maurice Wilson's diary: "Off again, gorgeous day."

Index

Printed in Great Britain
by Amazon